NOW THAT YOU CAN INVEST LIKE A PRO

MORE PRINCIPLES AND STRATEGIES FOR BUILDING WEALTH

LIKE THE WORLD'S GREATEST INVESTORS

JAMES PATTERSENN JR.

This book was published for educational purposes, and it's not intended to provide specific personalized advice. It's sold with the understanding that the author or publisher is not engaged in rendering legal, accounting, investment or other professional services. Investing in stocks and the stock market involves varying degrees of risk, and there's no assurance that a specific stock, investment principle or investment strategy will be profitable for an individual, group or organization. All information contained in this book was gathered from sources believed to be reliable, but neither the author nor the publisher can accept responsibility for its accuracy.

The author or publisher specifically denies any responsibility for liability, loss, or risk, professional or otherwise, which is incurred as a consequence, directly or indirectly, of the use and application of any of the contents of this book.

Publisher's Cataloging-in-Publication Data

Names: Pattersenn, James, Jr., 1966- | Patterson, James Wade, Jr., 1966-

Title: Now that you can invest like a pro : more principles and strategies for building wealth like the world's greatest investors / James Pattersenn, Jr.

Description: Lancaster, SC : Trilogy Publishing Group, 2019. | Includes index. | Includes 9 charts. | Summary: Provides advanced strategies of the world's most successful investors.

Identifiers: LCCN 2019907050 | ISBN 9780989546447 (softcover)

Subjects: LCSH: Investments—United States. | Stocks—United States. | Investment analysis. | BISAC: BUSINESS & ECONOMICS / Investments & Securities / Analysis & Trading Strategies.

Classification: LCC HG4521.P38 N69 2019 | DDC 332.6 P3--dc23

LC record available at https://lccn.loc.gov/2019907050

CONTENTS

PART ONE

THINKING AND ACTING MORE LIKE A PRO!

INTRODUCTION

As I sit here, writing this introduction on this first day of June 2019, I have come to the profound realization that the principles and strategies of the world's greatest investors are as relevant now as they have ever been. While it is merely human nature to try and make some fast money or get-rich-quick, great investors such as John Bogle and Peter Lynch have warned us repeatedly against that type of thinking when it comes to investing in the stock market. Peter Lynch, having the great sense of humor that he does, has said that if we want to double our money quickly, fold it in half and put it back in our pocket. He made that comment many years ago and I think it still holds true today.

There's a lot of talk out there today in the media and among the economists, financial and investment experts, and a host of other experts about the probability of a recession in our near future. I've learned to tune them out; I've discovered that most of what they say isn't helpful to investors at all. After the completion of my first book, *You Can Invest Like a Stock Market Pro,* I realized that I still had so much information in my head that would be, unlike the media's advice, helpful to those small or individual investors. So, this book picks up where my first book left off and is a direct continuation of it. This book will look at additional principles and strategies that were not covered in my first book.

I think that it's a mistake for an individual to read one or two books on investing and then consider that's enough. As a matter of opinion, ten books or even twenty books would not be enough! Investing, like many other professions, is a lifelong learning process. *Now That You Can Invest Like A Pro* is meant to take you a little further along in your journey and to help you to become a better investor during your journey. It's also meant to prevent you from following the herd and to instruct you on how to zig when everyone else zags. I hope that this book does just that. So, let your learning be a lifelong endeavor.

CAN THE INDIVIDUAL OR SMALL INVESTOR REALLY BEAT THE MARKET

"Can the individual or small investor beat the stock market consistently?" is a question that has been asked, argued, and debated for about as long as the stock market has existed. To nobody's surprise, the issue has yet to be settled. Before attempting to answer that question, let's consider what the stock market is. When you hear individuals talking about outperforming the market, they are talking about the overall or broad stock market. The stock market is made up of institutional investors such as brokerage firms, investment banks, mutual funds, exchange-traded funds, and hedge funds and all of them have deep pockets for investment purposes. The market is also made up of the small or individual investor and investment groups whose pockets are not so deep. It's the institutional investors that own most of the market through their stock ownership and they are also the main driving force behind most of the stock market's movements or volatility. Because institutional investors are very wealthy and powerful entities, they can afford to recruit those they consider to be the best and brightest minds in finance and investing and to use the latest and best technology in hopes of obtaining their investing edge. Most people may not realize that most of the trading that takes place today is performed by computers with sophisticated software programs.

Now that you know what the market is, let's see what investors are really saying when they talk of beating the market. Generally, when we talk about beating the market, we are talking about earning investment returns higher than that of the S&P 500 Index which is a benchmark that mimics the return of the U.S. stock market as a whole. The S&P 500 Index is comprised of 500 large companies that are selected based on their size, liquidity, and sector that are supposed to provide a snapshot of the overall U.S. equity markets. S&P 500 Index funds are designed to match the return of the broad market. There are also many other funds that have been created to track a specific index such as the Dow Jones Industrial Average or the Wilshire 5000. In addition, many but not all exchange-traded funds (ETFs) are also designed to mimic an index or benchmark at minimal cost but to trade like stocks on an exchange.

For those individuals that don't have the time or desire to learn how to invest and to actively invest in the stock market through the selection of individual stocks, many investment advisors would recommend that they invest in index funds. By investing in index funds and exchange-traded funds, they are certain to closely match the return of the broader market or index that the fund is mimicking, and the performance will more than likely be better than that of most actively managed funds. The drawback to using index funds and exchange-traded funds is that those that mimic the broad market lose as much as the market does during a bear market and a little more once the small fees and expenses have been deducted. For example, during the period from 2000 through 2009, had you invested $10,000 into the S&P 500 Index at the beginning of the decade, that $10,000 investment was worth about $9000 at the end of the decade. Imagine that! Your money has been tied up and working for you for ten years only to be worth about 10% less in the end. That 2000 through 2009 period is known as the *Lost Decade,* and many financial experts are predicting this current decade to also be one of zero growth for both the economy and the stock market. If their dire predictions hold true, then those individuals or institutions owning index funds that represent the broad or overall market should only expect zero returns from their investments. I don't know of any investor that would willingly invest his or her money for ten years only to obtain zero growth and zero returns from it. That would be crazy; however, most predictions are usually wrong when it comes to the economy and the stock market.

It is estimated that more than ninety percent of fund managers and money managers fail to beat the returns of the broad market. Now, that may seem a little shocking to think that these highly intelligent and highly educated professionals can't beat the market and my belief that you and I can, may seem to be both a little ignorance and arrogance on my part. In addition, there are many voices out there telling us that we can't beat the market and are wasting our time trying to do so.

Sir John Templeton stated, "If you want to have better performance than the crowd (market), you must do things differently from the crowd." Oh, so it seems that if we ever hope to beat the market, we cannot think and act in the same manner that it does. Many years ago, Muhammad Ali, legendary boxer and three times Undisputed Heavyweight Champion of the World, was asked about his strategy against his opponents during boxing matches and his response was "I make them fight my fight." I was a teenager back then, and now that I'm much older, I realize that his response was genius. From the response of the master investors, we must never fight the market's fight, but we must fight our own fight as investors. Anand Chokkavelu of the Motley Fool wrote in an April 2010 article that "The best investors heed the experience and advice of past masters. The players, technologies, and market environment certainly change, but the basic secrets to beating the market largely stay the same." Warren Buffett, Peter Lynch, and numerous other great investors have said that the small or individual investor can beat the market over the long-term and with me, that's what counts. Could it be that all those pundits that can't beat the market themselves figure that since they can't, no one else can either? Even the amazing and energetic Jim Cramer of Mad

Money believes that the individual investors can beat the market by holding between five and ten stocks in their portfolio and then actively managing those positions.

I would rather take the advice of someone with a long-term track record of beating the market that tells me that I can too, instead of the advice of someone who hasn't and tells me that I can't. What about you? Finally, the best advice that I can offer here is to tell you not to focus on beating the market but to focus your time and effort into not becoming the market if you desire market-beating returns. If you don't have the time, patience, or inclination to learn how to invest successfully in individual stocks, it's probably best for you to simply stick to investing in index funds or exchange-traded funds.

INVEST LIKE THE MASTERS

Ric Flair, the professional wrestler, used to say, "To be the man, you've got to beat the man." When it comes to investing, there is a similar truth, and it is, "If you want to be a great investor, learn from the great investors." The principles and strategies of individuals such as John Templeton *(The Father of Global Investing)*, Peter Lynch, Warren Buffett & Charlie Munger (*The Dynamic Duo*), Benjamin Graham (*The Father of Fundamental Analysis* and *The Father of Value Investing*), John Bogle (*The Father of the Index Fund*), Charles Brandes, Philip Fisher, David Dreman, William Gross (*The Bond King*), Jim Slater *(The Warren Buffett of the United Kingdom)*, John Neff, Shelby C. Davis, Walter Schloss, and many other of the world's most successful investors were studied and went into the writing of this book. It would be a serious mistake for anyone that wants to be a better investor to fail to take advantage of the knowledge and insight that these investors possess.

Every once in a while, some investment experts will bash Warren Buffett and question his abilities and some of his investment decisions or stock picks, but they always end up looking a little silly in the end. These same investors have not even come close to obtaining the success that Buffett has achieved as an investor, yet they have the audacity to question his abilities as an investor. It's kind of like the black belt at the local karate school, who has never won any type of championship, telling Chuck Norris how to fight. Buffett has been one of the world's most successful investor for at least the past forty years. Many of those that have trusted Warren Buffett, Charlie Munger, and the other great investors have become millionaires and billionaires. There's another famous saying, "If you can't beat 'em, join 'em."

PRACTICING WHAT HAS BEEN PREACHED

Many financial experts, financial advisors, and seasoned investors teach others the right way to invest, but when it comes to adhering to the same rules and principles that they teach others, they fail to do so themselves. They convince themselves that they are smarter than everyone else that's investing in the stock market and that they can predict its movement. In the end, their investments perform no better than those of the average investor. Why? They fail to practice what they preach or teach. Make up your mind to not fall into that same trap. When you don't know what you are doing, it's very easy to lose money in the stock market. I learned that the hard way. About the dumbest thing that an individual could do is fail to listen to those stock market pros that have already succeeded at investing. Of all people, they would know what works and what doesn't.

One day I was exercising at a local fitness center, and there was this big, muscular guy working out also. His physique was beyond impressive, and I found myself watching how he trained in hopes that I would pick up some training knowledge that would make my workouts more productive. Not only did he have a physique that most men long for, but he also possessed almost inhuman strength to go with that physique. On this particular day, there was another fellow exercising. He was scrawny and could not have weighed more than 120 to 130 pounds, yet he proceeded to lecture the individual with the impressive physique about how to train. I could not believe it. The individual with the incredible physique immediately responded to him and said, "Look at you and look at me!" This drew everybody's attention in the gym. At that comment, the skinny guy was silenced and embarrassed, to say the least. So, what's my point? My point is that I will not be like the scrawny guy and fool myself into thinking more of myself than I ought to when it comes to investing, and neither should you. The road has already been paved by others long ago. The only thing that we need to do is get on it and ride. I believe in the principles and strategies taught by the great investors and follow them with great dedication because I'm determined to practice what they preached.

BUY AND HOLD DOES NOT MEAN BUY AND FORGET

It's my belief that to do well in the stock market, an investor must have the intention to invest for the long-term, and as they say, "stay the course." With that said, I must admit that it will not always be possible to hold a specific stock for several years. Things change, and sometimes they change quickly in business. Those changes can be good or bad, and it's the bad ones that will make you have to purge your portfolio of what appeared to have been an outstanding stock at the time of your purchase.

For example, several years ago, I really liked Aeropostale Inc. because it seemed to be the perfect company with a very impressive performance history when looking at the company's fundamentals. Because Aeropostale was such an impressive business, I wrote several articles about it and used it in many examples to describe the almost perfect investment. Since those earlier writings, I can only ask myself, "What happened to Aeropostale?" Aeropostale Inc. filed for bankruptcy in May of 2016 and is no longer a publicly-traded company but is owned by Simon Property Group and General Growth Properties. Recently, I visited a local mall with my granddaughters at their request, although I was reluctant to go. I'm not one that cares much for walking around a mall all day knowing that I'm not going to buy anything, but I realized that by going, it would give me the opportunity to check the foot traffic at the different retailers within the mall.

It's an idea I got from reading and studying the investment strategies of the great Peter Lynch. Upon watching Aeropostale for a while, I notice that it hardly had a customer in the fifth teen or twenty minutes that I monitored the store. I went next to American Eagle Outfitters, and it wasn't much better. In the end, I discovered that H&M and Foot Locker had more foot traffic than about every other business in that particular mall on both occasions that I visited it. My main point from all of this is never to buy a stock and just forget about it because businesses change, customers' desires change, management change, and it doesn't take long for something to happen that turns a good investment into a bad one. You, as an investor, must never develop the buy and forget mentality.

The world's greatest investors would never buy a stock and forget about it, and neither should we. Stay updated with events or circumstances surrounding every business that you are invested in. You need to know what's happening because doing so will allow you to make better decisions concerning your investments. In an article written by Jim Cramer that I read, he says that the individual investors can beat the market by holding between five and ten stocks in their portfolio and then actively managing those positions. Notice that he said, "actively managing those positions." If you are actively managing your stocks, you certainly can't be buying and forgetting. You are buying and paying attention. That's pretty much what the amazing Jim Cramer is telling us that we must do to be successful individual investors and coming from someone of his genius, you know that it's got to be good advice.

DON'T LET POOR SHORT-TERM PERFORMANCE SWAY YOU

It has been said again and again that the investor is usually his own worst enemy when investing in stocks. Why? Because most investors tend to sabotage their success through an unsuccessful program of flipping stocks as if they were houses or pieces of real estate. Stocks are not real estate, but their ownership entitles the investor to partial ownership of the business and some of the profits that it earns. In reality, every investor should see himself or herself as part-owner of the business for every stock that they own.

Most of today's investors invest with their emotions, and that type of investing has proven throughout history to be dangerous and usually leads to substantial losses of invested funds. This is true because today's investors get caught up in the short-term performance of their portfolios or the short-term performance of stocks within their portfolios. For example, an investor will usually buy stocks for his or her portfolio when the news is good, and a stock's price is climbing and will usually sell on bad news when the stock is falling or has fallen in price. This type of short-term trading is a loser's game. The Motley Fool Team says that an investor's minimum holding period for each stock that is purchased should be three to five years. If today's investors adhered to that recommendation, it would prevent them from being swayed by the poor short-term performance of their portfolios or of stocks within their portfolios. In the process of my investment research, I created several practice portfolios to test strategies used by some of the world's best and most successful investors. Here, I want to tell you about one specific portfolio. It's a practice portfolio that I created in October of 2007 before the Great Recession struck. Of course, I had no idea that we were about to enter a recession at the time, but I just felt that something wasn't right although I took no action. With this particular portfolio, I wanted to see how it would perform if I created it using some of the strategies outlined in my book titled *You Can Invest Like a Stock Market Pro.* I built the portfolio with what I considered to be overvalued stocks that lacked the important margin of safety, and the portfolio was to be a test in the extreme to see how the strategies would hold up under less than ideal purchase conditions. Thirteen stocks were picked for the portfolio on October 2, 2007. Here are the original stock symbols for those thirteen stocks: PPDI, PFE, OMC, LOW, HOG, CHS, BBY, BBBY, ARO, AEO, RYL, SEIC, BJS.

Now, here is what's amazing! The portfolio was down 45% or 50% at different points with every stock within the portfolio experiencing a loss, and most of the stocks experienced heavy losses of 25% or more from my pick price. At its eighth-year mark, the portfolio had a total gain of 31.5%. Pharmaceutical Product Development Incorporated (PPDI) was taken private in December of 2011. BJ Services Company (BJS) merged with Baker Hughes (BHI) in April of 2010. BHI shares were issued as the result of the merger. Of the twelve stocks that were still in the portfolio, nine gained and three lost money. Of the nine stocks that made money, the average gain stood at 57.8%, and of the three stocks that lost money, the average loss stood at 48%. As I stated earlier, the portfolio had a total gain of 31.5%. So, what's the main lesson to be learned from the results of that research? It's this. If you don't allow your portfolio's short-term performance to cause you to jump into and out of stocks or to flee the stock market altogether, you stand a good chance of making some money. In reality, you stand a good chance of making a lot of money, and this applies even when you have paid what appear to be high prices for the stocks within your portfolio. Now, I certainly don't want you to ever overpay for a stock, and only recommend that you buy a specific stock when the desired margin of safety is available. Again, remember that buy and hold never means to buy and forget. As I have learned from reading Jim Cramer's books, we must never buy and forget. We must buy and actively manage our portfolios if we want to achieve success as investors.

BLOGS FOR BETTER INVESTING AND FINANCES

We now live in a world that greatly relies on technology that takes on many forms with some of the more popular being cell phones, smart TV's, computers, the internet, the iWatch and now, self-driving cars. Yes, self-driving cars are on the way with many being tested in many parts of the United States and other countries too. Now, I want to talk about the cell phone for just a moment. I'm really amazed at the influence and hold that cell phones have on the world today. It seems as if most people cannot function without them. In the United States, we have become a nation that's hooked on cell phones. We are truly a nation of cell phone junkies. Even my granddaughters had cell phones at the early age of ten or eleven. Many years ago, it would have been unimaginable to think of a ten-year-old walking around with a cell phone and most ten-year-olds don't even have a job. The point that I'm making is that it's events of the sort that further prove that the information technology age is in full swing and has been so for some time now.

Now, I'm not against technology. In fact, I love it as most other intelligent, warm-blooded Americans do. What really intrigues me about this age is all the free educational information that can be obtained through internet access. Let me give you an example. The heater core in my vehicle started leaking water which caused my car to lose water over a period of a few days then the vehicle would run hot. Upon checking around, most mechanics wanted to charge me a small fortune to replace the leaking component. I was convinced that I would be better served by doing the repair job myself. According to the automotive repair manual that I referred to for my specific vehicle, replacing the heater core was a five to six-hour job. I thought to myself that there's got to be a better, easier, and faster way to replace the heater core. So, I searched the internet for the answer. Eventually, my search led me to YouTube© which actually walked me step-by-step by video through the replacement process and the estimated five to six-hour job was completed in about half the time. I saved some money because I didn't have to pay a mechanic and watching the repair video on YouTube didn't cost me one red penny. I realize that this book is about investing, not automotive repair. Just imagine how much very good and useful information can be obtained through the internet.

There are many great investors and financial experts out there that may not be well known to the world but have the ability to teach us how to succeed when it comes to our finances and investing. Trust me. They are out there, and we should make it our goal to find them and learn. Those individuals can put us on the right path to getting our finances in order, improving our credit, eliminating or reducing our debt, and building wealth through a program of common-sense investing. They are able to help us to look at ourselves and our finances in ways that we would never even consider. These amazing investors and financial experts usually have blogs that we can read and put to use free of charge. Once you have discovered those bloggers that you really like, you will realize that the time spent locating them was worth the small effort.

To get started, go to an internet search engine such as Google or Yahoo and type "investment blogs" or "financial blogs" into the search portal. Be sure to save those blogs that are of interest to you into your "favorite's folder." I have decided to provide you with a list of some of my favorite investing and financial blogs. These bloggers are some very intelligent and knowledgeable people that know what they are talking about. A list and description of some of my favorite bloggers follow next but you should know that the list is far from being complete.

***Abnormal Returns*, abnormalreturns.com**

Founded in 2005 by Tadas Viskanta, a private investor and investment author with decades of experience in the financial markets. *Abnormal Returns* is a web site that's dedicated to educating investors on how to obtain above average returns through a program of sound investment principles and strategies. You will find very interesting and educational articles on a variety of subjects and I think the articles are excellent. The web site also offers a free newsletter.

***Contrarian Edge*, contrarianedge.com**

Vitaliy Katsenelson is a value investor and published author. He is also the Chief Investment Officer at Investment Management Associates Inc., a value investment firm located in Denver, Colorado. Katsenelson writes articles on investing and I find his analyses of stocks to be interesting and intriguing. I think Katsenelson is one amazing and gifted individual and his amazing talent surfaces in those interesting and stimulating articles that he writes. I think that he inherited his talent and his quick-wittedness from his father who is a gifted artist. I know this because I have seen some of his paintings included with articles written by Mr. Katsenelson. *Contrarian Edge* also offers a free newsletter at the web site and I highly recommend that you subscribe to it.

***Crossing Wall Street*, crossingwallstreet.com**

This blog and web site was founded by Eddy Elfenbein to help individual investors. The web site has great articles and provides analyses of individual stocks. Elfenbein also presents a yearly buy list of stocks free of charge that has outperformed the S&P 500 over the most recent thirteen-year period. The total return of his buy list stands at 211.3% compared to a total return of 160.0% for the S&P 500 from 2006 through 2018. Every year there's always some picks on his buy list that excite me because they qualify as what I label as worry-free stocks. Mr. Elfenbein also offers a free subscription to the *CWS Market Review*.

***Investor Junkie*, investorjunkie.com**

Investor Junkie is dedicated to educating individuals about finance and investing. Its goal is to help individuals to become better investors and to help them achieve financial freedom through their investment activities. It's also a web site dedicated to helping individuals become better entrepreneurs. You will find excellent articles to guide you in the right direction when it comes to your finances and investing. *Investor Junkie* offers a free weekly newsletter.

Novel Investor, novelinvestor.com

Since its founding, the main focus of *Novel Investor* has been about the journey of learning and sharing timeless investment wisdom. Jon, the founder, uses his blog to document what he has learned and continues to learn throughout his investing journey since investing is a lifelong learning process. Charlie Munger and Warren Buffett, two of the world's most successful businessmen and investors, have demonstrated and proven the necessity of always learning to compound ones investing wisdom. *Novel Investor's* library contains interviews, speeches, case studies, research, books and much, much more that will help us on our journey. This is an outstanding blog that's very educational, and Jon also uses and recommends some great financial tools that will help you and me to become better investors. *Novel Investor* offers a free weekly newsletter.

***Old School Value*, oldschoolvalue.com**

Jae Jun, a value investor, founded *Old School Value* in 2007. The web site is loaded with outstanding articles and free tools to help you to succeed as an investor. Jun's analyses of various stocks are very detailed and informative, as is his overall knowledge about investing. I just love all the free investment tools offered at the web site in addition to the free weekly newsletter.

***Planting Money Seeds,* plantingmoneyseeds.com**

Planting Money Seeds is a finance and investment blog founded by Miranda Marquit. I find Marquit's articles to be straightforward and refreshing. She covers a variety of topics from budgeting to investing to help us grow our wealth. I think that Marquit is unpredictable and exciting with her blogs and I look forward to reading everything that she writes because I never know what to expect from her blogs and I just love them! Don't forget to subscribe to her free weekly newsletter.

***Retire by 40,* retireby40.org**

This blog was founded by Joe Udo in 2010 to keep a tab of his early retirement journey. Although this web site is dedicated to teaching others how to retire early, its articles on saving, investing, frugal living, etc., will greatly benefit anyone willing to put into action what is learned at this very educational blog. What's even more exciting is the fact that Mr. Udo is living proof that early retirement is possible and to be able to retire by 40, is downright impressive.

***Value Walk,* valuewalk.com**

Value Walk is an interesting blog and web site founded by Jacob Wolinsky in 2010. *Value Walk* is dedicated to teaching the principles of value investing, but you will find articles on a variety of subjects, profiles of famous investors, and some very good stock screens at the web site. *Value Walk* also offers a free newsletter.

PART TWO

MORE PRINCIPLES & STRATEGIES OF THE INVESTMENT PROS

ASSET ALLOCATION

In 2008 and 2009 many of the asset allocation strategies used by investors to mitigate risk and improve returns within their portfolios did not perform as expected. Even the portfolios of some of the best investors in America suffered losses in the 30% to 50% range. Berkshire Hathaway's Class A shares fell 32% in 2008 and were down almost 50% during the financial panic that set in during the early part of 2009.

To explain to you what asset allocation means, I decided to provide you with a good definition provided by Investopedia. Here is Investopedia's definition:

Asset allocation is an investment strategy that attempts to balance risk versus reward by apportioning a portfolio's assets according to an individual's goals, risk tolerance, and investment horizon.

Let me be clear here. This is not a book about asset allocation. There are, no doubt, many books written on the subject but one book that I find to be very interesting is *The Alternative Answer* written by author and investment advisor Bob Rice. In it, Rice instructs investors on how to create investment portfolios that also takes advantage of alternative investments that were until recently only available to the wealthy. The ultimate goal of the book is to show investors how to use nontraditional options to significantly increase returns while reducing the risk of large losses such as those obtained by many investors in 2008 and 2009. In *The Alternative Answer,* Rice goes into great detail explaining options such as hedging strategies, private equity, venture funding, managed futures, master limited partnerships, farmland, timber, infrastructure, peer-to-peer lending, Treasury Inflation Protected Securities, and many other nontraditional strategies. think that *The Alternative Answer* is an excellent book and I recommend that any investor that's interested in the subject of Asset Allocation take some time to read it.

The reason that I'm not concerned with asset allocation is because I maintain a concentrated portfolio of twenty stocks or less, and the truth is that the longer I invest, the more I lean to desiring a portfolio of lesser and lesser stocks. By maintaining a concentrated portfolio, it's easier to get to know each business better and easier to actively manage each position within the portfolio. An investor is always better off with fewer positions that he or she knows well than a lot of positions that he or she knows very little about. I believe that having a very good understanding of each of your investments goes a long way toward reducing risk.

I realize that a carefully planned and executed asset allocation strategy could be of benefit to most investors. I see nothing wrong with an investor making it a very important part of his or her investment strategy. Since I strongly believe in keeping my portfolios concentrated in the number of stocks that they contain, I have little desire to implement an asset allocation strategy in them. In addition, I do not invest in commodities except through common stocks. I will leave you with a very intelligent recommendation made to investors by the legendary investor, Jim Slater. He has said that regardless of what an investor believes that the stock market is going to do, an investor should always stay at least 50% invested in the stock market. Like Slater, I believe that staying at least 50% invested in the stock market is a wise and prudent thing to do regardless of the asset allocation strategy that an investor chooses to use.

DIVIDENDS: YOU CAN HAVE YOUR CAKE AND THE ICING TOO!

Dividends are the profits that are earned on a stock or other investment that are returned to investors in the form of a cash payment or stock shares. They should be a vital part of the wealth building process for the investor, but I do not include dividends when valuing a stock or performing a stock analysis and my reason is simply that dividends can be cut. The Great Recession has proven that. Also, a lot of fast-growing companies tend not to pay dividends but will usually retain earnings and reinvest them back into the business. This is especially true with small to mid-sized businesses. By not including dividends, I'm able to value all investments on the same merits.

Most importantly, I believe that every investor should strive to achieve superior returns even before dividends are included. Suppose that I purchase a stock that provides a return of 20% annually, not including dividends. A 20% return is nothing to shake a stick at; however, the stock also pays a 3% dividend which I have not even considered since it may be reduced or cut out. The inclusion of the dividend gives me a 23% annual return instead of the 20% that I was expecting. To put it another way, dividends should be the icing on the cake, but I want you to make sure that the cake is so good that I would eat it even if it had no icing on it. In his book, *Common Stocks and*

Uncommon Profits, Philip A. Fisher had this to say about dividends, "Actually dividend considerations should be given the least, not the most weight by those desiring to select outstanding stocks. Perhaps the most peculiar aspect of this much-discussed subject of dividends is that those giving them the least consideration usually end up getting the best dividend return."

BUILDING A STOCK'S POSITION WITHIN YOUR PORTFOLIO

The question has been asked again and again about the best strategy or method to use when adding a new stock position to an investment portfolio. Some professionals believe that the entire sum of money to be invested should be spent all at once for the purchase. In other words, some believe in a one-time lump sum purchase. Other professionals believe that an investor should gradually build a position for each new investment through a program of *dollar cost averaging* or by splitting the purchases up. Here's a definition of dollar cost averaging:

The process of investing a fixed amount or percentage of money into an investment at regular intervals regardless of the investment's cost.

According to research, lump sum investing will usually produce a higher return than dollar cost averaging about 7 times out of 10. The drawback to investing a lump sum into a particular investment is that the investment could experience a significant drop in price soon after its purchase. I must admit that I'm no stranger to such an event happening to me on several occasions. Let me tell you about just one of my experiences. Many years ago, I spent a lump sum of more than $5000 buying shares of First Marblehead Corporation only to watch the stock tumble in price, turning my investment into less than $2000 in only a few weeks. In the end, I lost most of my money on that investment. Had I split my purchases up over a few months or weeks,

I would have become suspicious of the sudden drop in my shares' price and would have at the very least reassessed the situation and my reason for purchasing First Marblehead. I also would have held off purchasing more shares of the stock until I had a better picture of what was going on with the company and more than likely would have only lost about one-third of the money that I lost. I eventually drew the conclusion that First Marblehead was a financial stock that got crushed along with all other financial stocks during the brutal 2008-2009 period of the Great Recession. In the end, the business never recovered and was taken private. Fortunately for me, I held the stock long enough to offset the loss with capital gains from some other investments. So, I don't mind telling you that I'm not a big fan of the strategy of investing a lump sum into a stock or any other security sold in the market.

Dollar cost averaging, unlike investing a lump sum, reduces the risk of investing a large amount of money into an investment at the wrong time, and through its use, an investor will buy more shares at lower prices and fewer shares when prices are higher. There has been a considerable amount of controversy concerning dollar cost averaging, but I believe that it is especially useful for employees that invest through 401Ks and other types of employer-sponsored retirement plans. Once the retirement account is set up, the employer deducts contributions from the employee's check during each pay period which makes the process automatic and makes it easier for even the undisciplined saver to build wealth. Another advantage to dollar cost averaging is the fact that it allows an individual to invest small sums of money into the stock market since most individuals probably don't have lump sums of money to invest. In time, the investor that sticks to a steady plan of dollar cost averaging is likely to have a substantial nest egg when the time comes to retire.

Although I'm for dollar cost averaging, I don't believe that it should be used to invest in individual stocks. The wise investor should only be buying stocks that trade at a discount to their fair or intrinsic value. With mutual funds, bond funds, index funds, exchange-traded funds and some other types of securities, intrinsic value is usually not an issue for the investor, however, intrinsic value is at the heart of successfully investing in individual stocks. Because of the importance of intrinsic value, I like the method that Jim Cramer, an investment genius and the host of *Mad Money,* uses to build his positions when investing in individual stocks although I use a slightly modified version of his method. By the way, if you don't believe that he's a genius, just watch him in action on *Mad Money* and I'm convinced that you will change your mind. If the man talks in his sleep, I can guarantee you that it's about stocks. What an amazing and energetic individual Mr. Cramer is but according to his books, Mrs. Cramer is the amazing one. Now, let's take some lessons from a master of the market.

I use to think that it was quite ridiculous to build a position in a stock by spreading purchases out over a few periods instead of one lump sum investment because I believed that the individuals that bought in such a manner really didn't know the value of what they were buying. Now, I gladly admit that I was wrong in my belief. Especially, after watching some of my lump sum investments head south for the winter. In Cramer's book, *Jim Cramer's Get Rich Carefully,* he stresses the importance of an investor splitting his or her purchases up when starting a position in a new stock. He says that doing so gives an investor the opportunity to lower his cost basis with each purchase. Let's put it another way, he believes that every time an investor purchase shares of a particular stock, he or she should attempt to purchase those shares cheaper, thereby, lowering the average cost per share that is paid for the shares. Cramer also teaches that after the initial purchase, an investor should only buy more shares when he or she can lower their per share cost basis by a full point or $1. A "point" is the terminology used to express a $1 price change in the value of a stock. If you were able to purchase a stock ten points lower, it means that you purchased each share $10 lower or that you lowered you per share cost basis by ten points. With me, before I make my second and third purchase, I like to wait to see if the stock will drop a few more dollars although I'm willing to pay my determine purchase price which is a discounted price of the stock's intrinsic value. I will always determine the intrinsic value of a stock and then I will discount the stock for risk. With me, it may mean waiting a few weeks or months before buying more shares. If the stock falls a few more dollars, I buy more shares and if it does not, I will still buy more shares for my portfolio as long as I'm able to purchase the shares at my desired discounted price. If I'm unable to build a sizeable position of a stock within my portfolio because the stock becomes too expensive, I continue to hold onto the smaller lot as I would any other shares and will usually only sell my shares in accordance to sell rules that I have established for myself. It's as simple as that for me.

Some may argue that using such a strategy will sometimes prevent you from building a decent position in a stock that experiences a swift and serious run-up in price and that's true, but from my experiences, most of the stocks that I buy usually fall further in price over a period of several months before their prices stabilize or begin to recover. That drop in the price is now something that I have come to expect after my stock purchases and you would be wise to expect the same. I have not always thought this way, but now believe that the investor that split his purchases up and buys more shares of a stock when he or she is able to lower the cost basis of the shares with each purchase is investing intelligently since doing so will lower the average cost per share each times shares are added to the portfolio. A lump sum purchase of our shares will leave us with no wiggle room to lower our average cost per share if the shares were to drop in price. So, I'm simply in agreement with what Jim Cramer teaches us through his program, *Mad Money* and his investment books. Splitting our purchases up over three to four buy periods is the best way to buy individual stocks, and I think that more money will be made and less will be lost through the process.

Is there a situation in which I will perform lump sum purchases? Yes. I will perform them with stocks that are available at an estimated discount of

50% or more off of their fair value. I figured some time ago that stocks trading at such a big discount are such a bargain that they are unlikely to fall much further before being recognized by the investment community for the bargains they really are. I recently discovered that the legendary Kahn Brothers like to start out by buying a small stake in any stock that they are purchasing instead of buying all at once. They have a few reasons for doing so. The first is that shares that they buy frequently go down in price before going up. Sounds just like my situation, doesn't it? They also believe that by starting out with only a small stake in the business, it gives them the opportunity to get to know the company better before investing a large amount of capital into its stock.

Summary

1. The biggest risk of investing a lump sum into an individual stock is the fact that the stock could experience a big drop in its price soon after it has been purchased.

2. Dollar cost averaging reduces the risk of investing a large amount of money into an investment at the wrong time.

3. Dollar cost averaging is especially effective for employees that invest through 401Ks and other types of employer-sponsored retirement plans.

4. Intrinsic value or fair value is at the heart of investing successfully in individual stocks.

5. When adding a new stock position to your portfolio, divide your purchases up over three or four buy periods unless the stock is available at a discount of 50% or more off of its intrinsic value. When shares are available at a discount of 50% or more off of its intrinsic value, consider purchasing them with one lump sum investment.

6. After your initial purchase of shares, attempt to buy more shares when you are able to lower the average cost per share that you pay for your shares and never pay above your determined purchase price for new shares.

7. If a stock takes off after your initial purchase and you are unable to buy additional shares at your determined purchase price, continue holding onto the smaller lot and sell only when it makes sense to do so, such as when the shares reach their intrinsic value or become overvalued.

SPECULATING: WHEN INVESTING ISN'T INVESTING

I was initially reluctant to write about speculating since I was unsuccessful at it. Oh yes! I have a few years of experience at speculating with stocks although I had no idea of what it was called at the time. To make matters worse, I combined my speculating activities with the strategy of day trading. I now compare the two when combined with the equivalency of two loaded locomotives headed for a head-on collision. Once they collide and the smoke and dust clears from the accident, what you've got left is one big mess to clean up. Even with my reluctance, I thought that it still makes sense to talk about speculating since there will be some that read this book that are probably speculating, others that are curious about it, and still others that are doing it but don't know that they are. By the way, on a scale from one to ten, I rate myself a zero when it comes to speculating and doing so successfully. Yes, I know that zero isn't on a scale from one to ten. It used to be that after my experience speculating, if I heard mention of the term "speculating" in relations to investing, it was taboo for me. I wanted nothing else to do with it and for me to even consider it was a big no-no!

Did you know that up until the 1920s all stocks or equities were considered purely speculative? Only bonds were considered to be authentic investments. In those days, an investment was defined as something that paid the investor and since bonds paid dividends, they were considered the only legitimate investments when it came to the markets. Well, times have changed and so has the meaning of some terms. I decided to check Investopedia to find out a modern definition of speculating and Investopedia defines it in the following manner:

"The act of trading an asset, or conducting a financial transaction that has a significant risk of losing most or all of the initial outlay in expectation of significant gain."

It's the last part of that definition that makes speculating so enticing and that's the prospect of significant gain. In an article titled *Intelligent Speculation Is a No-Brainer,* written by value investor Sham Gad, he states "Ben Graham, author of the classic investing book *The Intelligent Investor,* said that if you are not investing, you are speculating. What gets folks in trouble is that they think they are investing but in fact are speculating. An investment operation is defined by three characteristics: diligent analysis, margin of safety, and adequate return. Without those three conditions, you are making a speculative bet." That statement says a lot. All three characteristics must be present for investors to have a sound methodology in place for investing, thereby increasing their opportunities for success and the lack of any one element leads to speculating at best.

When we consider gambling, it is based purely on chance. For example, once a gambler rolls the dice, he has no control over what numbers the dice will land on. Although the risk can be calculated, what the gambler is really depending on is some good luck or momentum. Speculators also take calculated risks. The risks are very high but so is the payoff if they are right. According to a Motley Fool's article written by Kingkarn Amjaroen, the main driving force for speculation is a person's desire to get rich quickly. This same mindset is what leads many investors to make poor investment decisions and choices that have not been thought through or planned that eventually lead to the poor performance of their investments. Many of them think that they are investing when, in fact, they are speculating and don't even realize it. Up to this point, I know that I have had nothing positive to say about speculating. Now, let me let you in on a shocker. Many of the world's most successful investors speculate with some of their investment picks. Quality Systems, Pier 1 Imports, Medifast Inc., and Almost Family Inc. are successful companies today that certainly were considered stock speculations by most experts several years ago. I found that even Green Mountain Coffee Roasters was once a speculative stock and could have been purchased for less than one dollar per share in December of 1999. When I sold Green Mountain Coffee Roasters, it had changed its name to Keurig Green Mountain Inc. My average cost for my shares was $19.89 and my average selling price was $131.36 giving me a total return of 560.4% if my math is correct. Not a bad return from a stock that at one time was considered speculative. Just imagine if we could have bought a few thousand shares of the stocks just mentioned when they were still in their infancy. We would have without exaggeration become super rich. With stocks, your loss stops at zero if you are not buying on margin, but if the stock takes off, it could be the next Oracle, Wal-Mart, or Starbucks. Knowing this to be the case is why even many of the great investors speculate within their portfolios.

As further proof that even the world's best investors speculate, visit the web site Gurufocus.com. Once there, click on the names of a few of the guru investors (another name for great investors or master investors) listed at the site. Once you click on a name, pull up the portfolio of the investor and take a look at his or her stock holdings. While still at the same site, click on the stock symbols for those stocks contained in the portfolio of the investment guru and you will also be able to pull up financial information for those individual stocks. Go ahead and pull it up. You may have to check several stocks or go through a few investors, but I bet that it won't take long to retrieve some stocks that will shock you. After you recover from the shock, you will ask yourself "Why in the world would these smart guys and gals invest in the stocks of businesses with such terrible fundamentals?" I'm convinced that the answer is "speculation" for some of those stocks. Especially when we consider what characteristics are necessary for an action to be considered investing: diligent analysis, margin of safety, and adequate return. Referring to Gurufocus.com, here are some well-known guru investors that I believe speculate within their portfolios: George Soros, Carl Icahn, Ken Fisher, Charles Brandes, Joel Greenblatt, Prem Watsa, Bruce Berkowitz, Julian Robertson (The Wizard of Wall Street), and John Paulson. Remember, these people know what they are doing when it comes to investing or speculating and are the best in the world at it. They won't always make money on their buys, but when they do, they make lots of it.

Now the truth is out that some of the world's greatest investors speculate, but you should know that they do so intelligently through what is referred to as *intelligent speculation.* Let's refer back to the article written by Sham Gad that I mentioned earlier for a better explanation. In the article, Gad states "investors can make intelligent speculative bets provided they have a clear understanding of what they are engaging in." Gad goes on to say, "speculation can still involve diligent research and analysis and what you give up in safety margin is made in return." Bernard Baruch was one of America's greatest and most successful speculators and there's no doubt that he used intelligent speculation. For example, listen to a few of his investment rules taken from his book *Baruch: My Own Story.*

- Don't try to buy at the bottom and sell at the top. This can't be done except by liars.
- Always keep a good part of your capital in cash. Never invest all your funds.
- Learn how to take your losses quickly and cleanly. Don't expect to be right all the time.

It's amazing to think that rules taught by a speculator born in 1870 are still applicable today whether you are an investor or a speculator. If after reading this section some of you are still interested in speculating and I know that some of you will be, you might as well know some of the trading rules used by some of the great speculators (past and present) and many of these same rules also apply to investing.

1. Know when you are speculating and when you are investing.
2. Realize that speculating is hard work. Nothing worth having comes easy.
3. Never trust forecasts. Most forecasters are lousy at their job.
4. Embrace volatility and use it to your advantage.
5. Don't mistake luck for success. Even the worst investors and speculators get lucky sometimes.
6. Never buy a stock because its price has decreased from a previous high.
7. Keep your emotions out of your decisions and stick to the facts at hand.
8. Have realistic expectations.
9. Use stop losses and stick to them.
10. Diversify because it does matter. It has been said that it's the only free lunch.
11. Don't try to time the stock market. The task is almost impossible.
12. Never act on hot tips from others. Always do your own homework.
13. Never build a position in a stock all at once. Split your purchases up.
14. Always analyze your buys and sells to see what you did wrong and what you did right.
15. If you are not an expert at speculating, only allocate a small percentage of your portfolio to speculating.

16. Don't become your own worst enemy. Self-sabotage is common in investing and speculating.

17. Don't buy too many securities. Stick with a few positions that you know well.

18. Always expect the unexpected.

I think that it's important that you know that there's nothing wrong with speculating if that's what you want to do, and you really understand what you are doing. Like investing, it's also a legitimate method to use when attempting to build wealth. You should just understand that it's a very risky practice. In Jim Cramer's book, *Jim Cramer's Get Rich Carefully,* he addresses speculation and gives some excellent advice on how to speculate and to do so intelligently and successfully. If you are serious about it, get his book and check it out. I recently read the book and think that it's outstanding and loaded with good information that you won't find anywhere else. Knowing what I now know, would I speculate again? Absolutely, but only with a small percentage of my portfolio and would stick to those stocks being bought by several master investors after I have done my own homework.

On a final note, in modern times, it's George Soros that's considered by many to be the greatest speculator alive on earth today. In 1973 he established the Quantum Fund and headed the fund for 26 years. During that period, he achieved a cumulative annual return of 32%. To this day, his fund's performance has been unmatched, and he is recognized as having the best performance record of any investment fund in the world. Soros is one of the richest men on earth with an estimated net worth of more than $8 billion dollars after having donated more than $32 billion to his philanthropic agency, Open Society Foundations. It's not luck or chance, but his knowledge that has made him the success that he is today.

MANAGING TWO OR MORE INVESTMENT PORTFOLIOS

In my mind, it's enough of a challenge to properly manage one investment portfolio especially when it also contains several individual stocks in it. From my experience, it seems best if the individual investor owns only one investment portfolio that he or she has to manage. Of course, I have come to realize that some things are not always that simple. For good reasons, it's common for millions of Americans to own two or more investment portfolios. It's not that hard for any of us to end up in that situation. Currently, I actually own and manage four investment portfolios and two of the portfolios contain only individual stocks in them. What I'm about to say next is the essence of what this section is about.

If you own two or more investment portfolios, be sure not to create duplicate portfolios or duplicate transactions by adding the same stock picks to each portfolio. Exactly what am I saying? Let's look at an example of what I'm talking about. If an investor has two portfolios and each portfolio contains ten stocks, he or she should make sure that none of the same stocks are contained in both portfolios. In other words, the investor should own a total of twenty different stocks between the two investment portfolios. Is there a good reason for recommending this method when managing two or more investment portfolios? Yes! Let's pretend that you currently own two investment portfolios (if you really don't) and that within those portfolios you own Jed Oil Company (bankrupt and no longer in business). Since Jed Oil is an oil company stock, you are certain that with fuel prices on a steady climb, you will make a good return on your investment. Not only that, you bought the stock with a strong conviction that it was an excellent pick. Several months later, you decided to check the price of Jed Oil Company and found that the stock had lost more than 90% of its value. To make matters worse, you remembered that you own Jed Oil shares in both of your investment accounts. When you and I own the same stocks in two or more accounts and the stocks turn out to be a doozy, it's like a *double whammy* (a situation in which two unpleasant events happen at the same time) for the investor. What if you own shares of that particular stock in three different accounts? Things get even worse!

What I'm telling you here, I learned from my own experiences managing more than one investment account. I don't care how great you may think a company or its stock is; limit your purchase of those shares to just one account. In doing so, you will be better diversified and will also avoid what it feels like to experience a double whammy. By the way, I lost a small fortune investing in Jed Oil. I was just getting started as a serious investor but had no idea of what I was doing when I bought it.

COATTAIL INVESTING

Coattail investing is the process of duplicating the trades of well-known and very successful investors. Coattail investing is nothing more than copycat investing. The coattail investor will make adjustments to his or her stock portfolio that corresponds to the changes made by the investor whose trades are being duplicated. The drawback to this style of investing is that the investor being duplicated may not practice a long-term buy and hold strategy, making it extremely difficult for others to accurately mirror changes that have been made to his or her portfolio. Although coattail investing may seem to be a very good investment strategy, it's not necessarily the best strategy for you and me. A stock that may be right for George Soros or Warren Buffett, may be wrong for us.

These individuals have such vast quantities of money to invest that they must invest in very large companies to see any type of meaningful returns on their investments. They have portfolios containing billions of dollars in stocks. As a matter of fact, George Soros and Warren Buffett manage more money than the amounts that exist in the economies of many small countries. The small investor has the advantage over these larger money managers because the small investor is able to find and purchase stocks of smaller companies that have lots of room for growth. Microsoft, Wal-Mart, Pfizer, and General Electric have not always been the large companies that they are today.

Although I'm not a strong advocate of coattail investing, I thought it would only be fair to tell you that one of the stocks that I sold out of one of my private portfolios was a coattail purchase. The purchase was USG Corporation, a construction materials supplier. Warren Buffett began buying USG Corporation in 2008 if I'm correct for about $46 to $47 per share. I knew that if Buffett was willing to pay that amount per share then the stock had to be worth a lot more. When the stock fell much lower in price during the Great Recession, I began to purchase shares for my personal portfolio at an average price of about $12 per share. I eventually sold my shares several years ago earning a very good profit in the process. When creating your own stock portfolio, I'm now convinced that coattail investing is not the best method for the individual or small investor. I think much better returns can be realized by selecting your stocks based on the stringent criteria such as the stress test explained in my first book titled *You Can Invest Like A Stock Market Pro* or from reading great books such as *One Up on Wall Street* written by Peter Lynch.

THE 50% SOLUTION

Believe it or not, the majority of investors that lose money do so because they fail to understand or to heed the 50% Solution. You may be asking yourself, "Exactly what is the 50% Solution?" In actuality, the 50% Solution has been around a long time and it originally applied to frugal living. It entailed using only half of what an individual normally would when it comes to consumer goods and thereby saving money since items would last longer. The 50% Solution has now been applied to dieting to lose weight and many other areas of life. For instance, with dieting, individual are to consume only half of what they would normally eat during meals and by doing they should lose weight since they would only be consuming about half the calories that they normally would.

Well, I think that the 50% Solution should also be applied to investing and, in our case, investing in stocks. Is it some type of magic formula for investing success? Oh, how I wish that it was! Peter Lynch has said, "The key to making money in stocks is not to get scared out of them." It's a known fact that most investors buy high and sell low. How can anyone ever expect to succeed as an investor with a strategy like that? The simple truth is that they won't. Now, let me tell you what I mean when I talk about the application of the 50% Solution to investing. It's the realization that any stock is subject to fall 50% or more in its trading price in any given year and sometimes for no apparent reason that makes sense to the investor. Again and again, research has indicated that those investors that continue to hold on to their investments for the long-term usually do quite well. Even with my own experience as an investor, I have found that about every stock that I have ever owned dropped in price after my purchase and some dropped significantly. If you and I have done our homework well, the 50% Solution simply means to continue holding our investments until the investment community eventually recognize their true value and push their prices up to their fair value and/or beyond. Even the legendary Warren Buffett has stated, "Unless you can watch your stock holdings decline 50% without becoming panic-stricken, you should not be in the market." I'm a witness that good stocks do recover, and many go on to reach new highs. So, the next time you purchase a stock or currently own stocks that fall or have fallen drastically in value, reflect on the 50% Solution before deciding to sell. Staying put may just be your best course of action.

PHILIP FISHER'S THREE-YEAR RULE

It's my greatest hope that at this point, you have learned the importance of investing long-term to improve your chances of investing successfully. When I consider the great investors, I cannot think of one that implements a short-term trading strategy. Since they don't, why should we?

Many years ago, it was common for the average investor to actually hold a stock for several years or invest for the long-term but it's unfortunate that those days are long gone. Long-term investing for many of today's investors may be considered a few hours, days, or weeks. In his book, *Common Stocks and Uncommon Profits,* investing pioneer Philip A. Fisher believed that if an investor had done his or her job correctly when purchasing common stock, that the time to sell was almost never. Fisher found that when investors held the right stocks for long periods of time, even in bad markets, they were usually rewarded with returns of several hundred or several thousand percent. Fisher was one who practiced what he preached by refusing to sell even those stocks from his portfolios that would have appeared to be overvalued by today's standards or measures. He held shares of Motorola for more than twenty-one years and in an interview said that he had held some stock shares a maximum of thirty years. Fisher found that those investors that sold very good stocks from their portfolios that they had perceived to be overvalued in an effort to buy them back once they had fallen in price usually didn't get the opportunity to do so. He found that those stocks often went on to reach new highs.

This section does not address the issue of when to sell a stock because that will be covered a little later. What this section is about is stressing the importance of having a long-term frame of mind when it comes to investing in individual stocks. More specifically, it's about having a Philip A. Fisher frame of mind when it comes to holding stocks.

In *Common Stocks and Uncommon Profits,* Fisher says that he established himself a three-year rule. Under his three-year rule, Fisher asked his clients whose portfolios he managed, to give him three years before judging his performance. He told them that if he had failed to produce satisfactory results for them at the end of three years, they should fire him. Now, I must admit that I have the slightest idea of what kind of performance Fisher or the clients expected. No doubt, it was some measure or goal that they had agreed to in advance. Fisher also applied his three-year rule to his management of individual stocks. When applied to stocks, he was determined to hold an individual stock for a minimum of three years regardless of how good or bad the stock had performed as long as nothing had happened to change his original view about the company. Even for those stocks that had risen significantly in price, he still adhered to his three-year rule.

From my research, I found some other great investors that also adhere to a three-year rule in a similar manner like Fisher. For example, the Motley Fool Team says that investors' minimum holding period for each stock that is purchased should be three to five years. As further evidence of support for the three-year rule, look at the following quote by great investor David Dreman, "If you have good stocks and really know them, you'll make money if you're patient over three years or more."

So, when I consider Fisher's three-year rule, I find that it makes a lot of sense. Even Warren Buffett sought out Philip A. Fisher for his knowledge about investing and said that he was as impressed by the man as by his ideas. If Fisher's three-year rule teaches us nothing else, it certainly teaches us the importance of patience when it comes to investing. There's no doubt that most investors could use a little more patience which is a necessity for successful investing, and it is patience that sets the world's greatest investors apart from the rest. So, I don't think we could go wrong with the implementation of Fisher's three-year rule into our investment plan or investment program.

WILLIAM O'NEIL'S 3 TO 1 PROFIT AND LOSS STRATEGY

In my research on investing, there have been times when I discovered information that got me really excited because it was almost too good to be true. As I read *The Successful Investor* written by legendary investor William O'Neil, I experienced such excitement on a few occasions, but what got me excited most was my reading of Step 2 titled *Use a Simple 3 to 1 Profit and Loss Plan.* First, O'Neil explains that the reason most investors lose a lot of money is because they don't know how to protect themselves from losses. Early in my investment career, I lost most of my money investing in stocks. My failure to protect myself from losses was definitely the main reason for my losses. Now, I include a margin of safety with every stock purchase along with several more important criteria to protect myself against those large catastrophic losses from which it's almost impossible to recover.

This section isn't about when to buy or sell but its intention is simply to open your eyes to another tool to put into your arsenal to protect yourself if you think that it's needed. In the section titled *The 50% Solution* which you should have already read at this point, I talked about the fact that stocks can fall 50% or more in any given year and sometimes investors will find no apparent reason for the fall. I certainly don't like to see any of my investments fall that much in price but as I write this section, I must admit that I have had a few stocks in my portfolios that are were down more than 50% from my average purchase price and like most investors and I didn't like it.

Remember, successful investing is also about thinking outside the box and using those principles and strategies that work for you. If you find that something doesn't work, don't use it. So, looking again at O'Neil's *3 to 1 Profit and Loss Strategy,* I find that in addition to protecting an investor from catastrophic losses that are hard to recover from, it also simplifies the decision of when to sell a stock. In his book, *The Successful Investor,* O'Neil states " I know of only one sure way, and that's to have a realistic plan of selling and taking profits on the way up, while a stock is still advancing, and selling and cutting every loss very short when a stock starts off poorly and goes against you." With O' Neil's *3 to 1 Profit and Loss Strategy,* the investor is to sell a stock that falls 7 or 8 percent below his or her purchase price without exception and O'Neil believes that by doing so, it will prevent the investor from suffering large losses from which he or she cannot recover. With the strategy, it is also recommended that an investor sell a stock when it has risen 20 to 25% above his or her purchase price. The strategy gets its name from the 3 to 1 ratio that is maintained between the 7 to 8% sell recommendation for losses and the 20 to 25% sell recommendation for taking profits.

Here's what's really amazing about the strategy. According to O'Neil, an investor can be wrong about 70% of the time on his or her stock purchases and still not get into any real trouble. That means that if an investor can improve on his or her stocks picks and pick winners more than 30% of the time they would probably do alright. What if the investor can pick winners 50% of the time? If that's done, we're talking about making some serious money. It is my hope that with the help of information contained in this book along with my other book titled *You Can Invest Like a Stock Market Pro*; the investors can pick winners more than 50% of the time. If Mr. O'Neil says that the strategy works then he should know because he has more than 40 years of trial-and-error experience with investing and if there were such a thing as an Investor's Hall of Fame, he would certainly have been inducted long ago. Now, am I saying that you should implement O'Neil's *3 to 1 Profit and Loss Strategy*? Not really but I'm not telling you not to either. I believe that the strategy could be an effective tool for the investor if some slight modifications are made. The way I figured it, to sell a stock at a 7 to 8 % loss means that the "stop-loss" would need to be used although I can't specifically recall O'Neil mentioning it in *The Successful Investor.*

I have already told you that most of the stocks that I purchase have a tendency to fall further in price after my purchase before recovering and the truth be told, some fall a lot further than I like. I have learned to accept that drops in prices are going to happen regardless of the investment methodology that an investor chooses to use. Because of great web sites such as Gurufocus.com and Insidermonkey.com, we are able to look at the actual portfolios of the great investors that are living and still actively investing today. We also have the opportunity to look at the performance of individual stocks and other securities contained in their portfolios. I have looked at many portfolios of these amazing men and women, and I have found that even the portfolios of investors of the caliber of Carl Icahn and Seth Klarman contain stocks that have taken a serious tumble in price with some of their stocks down more than 50% at some point.

Warren Buffett has stated, "Unless you can watch your stock holdings decline 50% without becoming panic-stricken, you should not be in the market." For those to whom his statement applies, I believe the use of the stop-loss is the answer. Maybe not in the 7 to 8% range as O'Neil suggests but a bit higher because of the volatility of stocks and of the stock market in general. The stop-loss is an automatic trade order placed with a broker to sell a security once it reaches a specified price or percentage change in order to limit an investor's loss on a security position.

In the 1950s, a little known investor named Nicolas Darvas started investing with only a few thousand dollars and turned that small investment into more than $2 million during a period of 18 months from when he first successfully applied what he called his *Techno-Fundamentalist Theory* of stock investing. With his theory, Darvas successfully used the stop-loss as his only defense against catastrophic losses and more specifically, he used the trailing stop-loss which is a stop-loss that increases by a specific amount or a specific percentage along with a stock's increase in price. As Darvas put it, "As to my basic strategy, I decided I would always do this: I would just jog along with an upward trend, trailing my stop-loss insurance behind me."

Although Jim Slater, *The Warren Buffett of the U.K.*, relied on a low PEG ratio to provide him a margin of safety against catastrophic losses, in his book *Beyond the Zulu Principle,* he had this to say about the stop-loss, "Many commentators recommend stop-loss systems and if this is going to make you sleep better, by all means, use one." Slater went on to suggest that the investor could set his or her stop-loss 20% below the highest price registered by the shares.

I must admit, the use of the stop-loss is something that's new to me and I'm still learning from it. The investor using the stop-loss could also combine it with a strict sell rule as O'Neil does but wait for a more significant price increase in a stock before selling such as when a gain of 50% or more has been obtained. The biggest argument against the use of the stop-loss is that the use of the stop-loss can result in an investor prematurely selling a stock that recovers and goes on to perform very well. I can attest to the fact that I have prematurely sold several stocks that went on to climb 100% or more in price and I did so without the use of the stop-loss. Selling to early happens to the best of investors. I have watched many interviews of some of the world's most successful investors, and when some were asked about their biggest investment mistakes, the response on several occasions was "selling to early". It's going to happen sometimes.

MERGERS AND ACQUISITIONS: WIN-LOSE SITUATIONS

Mergers or acquisitions can be a blessing or a curse. In other words, the investor may make money from them or he or she may lose money as a result of them. Let's first look at definitions of both types of transactions before we go any further:

A merger is the process or act of combining two or more businesses into one. An acquisition is the process or act of one business purchasing another business.

Regardless of which of the predicaments that you find yourself in with a business whose shares you own, money can be made or lost. Unfortunately, the investor with few total shares in comparison to the total number of shares outstanding has very little say as to whether or not a merger or acquisition is approved. Of course, as part owner, the investor's voice is through the vote granted by his or her share ownership.

As of now, I don't think that I have owned any shares in companies that have participated in any types of mergers during my ownership so I will not talk about mergers because I have no experience with them. I have held shares in some businesses that were acquired by other businesses at the time of my ownership. Since that's the case, I will only talk about acquisitions.

Most of the time when it is announced that one business plans to acquire another at a specific price, the shares of the business being acquired tend to move quickly to within close proximity to the agreed upon acquisition price. A good example of what I'm talking about happened to me. Komatsu Ltd. announced on July 21st, 2016 that it had agreed to acquire Joy Global Inc. for $3.7 billion or $28.30 per share and that the transaction should be completed by the middle of 2017. Pre-announcement, Joy Global's shares were trading in the $22-$23 range. Immediately after the acquisition was announced, shares of Joy Global climbed above $28 per share and were likely to continue trading within that range up to the completion of the acquisition. Acquisitions may appear to be a good thing, but the truth depends on what the investor paid for his or her shares of the business being acquired. For instance, looking back at Joy Global, I found that its shares traded as high as $101 during its most recent five-year period prior to the announcement , and its shares traded at a low of $8.35 during the same period. Those shareholders who bought in at the top and whose average cost per share was higher than the $28.30 probably were not too happy about Joy Global being acquired, and although I sold my shares at a small profit, neither was I. Those investors that got in at the bottom, especially those that purchased their shares when they were trading in the $8 per share range had something to be happy about. A 250% return in such a short period was something to be celebrated.

When the CEO and the Board of Directors agree to allow a business that they are running to be acquired by another business, I'm willing to bet that none of them are going to lose money. Just think, they would be totally against the acquisition if they were going to lose money in the process. The more likely scenario is that they are going to make money and lots of it even if the majority of their shareholders lose money from the acquisition. It seems to me that acquisitions are a win-win situation but only for those top executives and directors that are responsible for overseeing and making key acquisition decisions. Throughout my short career as an investor, there seem to be only two investors who pay such a good premium to shareholders during acquisitions that it's a win-win situation for everyone involved. They are the amazing and dynamic team of Charlie Munger and Warren Buffett. I want you to especially remember that you may find that a business whose shares you own announcing some type of merger or acquisition because it does happen sometimes. Just know also that unless you own a large percentage of shares, there's not much that you can do about the merger or acquisition and your main voice will be through the voting of your shares. Even then, the majority shareholders, those who own and control most of the company's stock, have more than likely told management that they are on board for the merger or the acquisition which pretty much cancels out your vote. Even then, all is not lost because if the management team is investor-oriented, they will attempt to receive a high enough premium during the acquisition or merger so that the majority of their investors make money.

USING THE DISCOUNTED CASH FLOW METHOD TO VALUE A STOCK

There is no doubt many different ways that investors use the *discounted cash flow method* to determine a stock's fair value, but I will show you how I use it in my attempt to determine a stock's fair value. I have no desire to know all the different manners or methods of calculating the discounted cash flow of a company, I want one effective method that works. What I'm going to show you has worked very well for me. Let's begin with an explanation of the discount cash flow.

The discount cash flow is a valuation method that gives us an estimate of a stock's fair value based on its future earnings per share estimates. After the earnings have been estimated, they are discounted to take into account the time value of money.

For example, if we believe that a specific stock will earn $5 per share exactly five years from now, we want to take into account that the $5 in earnings will be worth less in five years than it's worth today because of inflation and other factors. Since that's the case, we want to pay a discounted value for the stock that takes inflation, risk, and other factors into consideration.

I will use the abbreviation DCF to represent "discount cash flow" throughout my writings because it's a heck of a lot easier than typing the entire term out. What makes the DCF method of importance to me is the fact that I'm able to obtain yearly earnings estimates many years into the future through its use. In other words, I'm able to obtain a snapshot or picture of a stock's expected earnings per share for a certain number of years into the future that I specify. I do limit future earnings per share estimates to ten years. It is possible to estimate earnings further into the future but doing so is a recipe for disaster. Especially, when we really don't know what condition any company or business will be in within the next ten years. That's why the numbers that the DCF method provides are just estimates. Actual earnings per share may be higher or lower than the estimates that we obtain from our calculations. Regardless, I think that you will find the DCF method very helpful during the stock valuing process.

When I was first learning to use the DCF method, I did all of my calculations by hand. The calculations are not complex, but they are very time consuming without the use of a calculator created specifically for that purpose. Luckily for you and me, things have changed since then. There are numerous web sites with DCF calculators on them, but I have only found a few sites that are my favorites. It is my hope that the calculators are still available for many years to come because they save so much time compared to doing the discount cash flow calculations by hand. It probably takes me about fifteen to twenty minutes to perform a calculation by hand, but less than one minute using an online calculator. Needless to say, it has been many years since I have performed a discount cash flow calculation by hand, and I plan to keep it that way. Since I rely on online calculators to perform my calculation, it's the method that I will be explaining to you.

There are two online calculators that work for me, and I recommend that you check them out. There are others out there, but their intrinsic value or fair value estimates tend to be very high. My recommendation is that you use the DCF calculators located at Moneychimp.com and Gurufocus.com. The calculator located at Moneychimp.com is my absolute favorite and it's the one that I have mostly used. Keep in mind that other very good calculators may become available after this section is written or after this book has been published. So, keep a look out for them.

First, I will explain how to find the DCF calculator at Gurufocus.com. You will need to go online using Google or another web browser of your choice. Once at the browser, type "gurufocus.com" into the search portal of the browser and click the "search" button and "GuruFocus.com" should appear as the first selection on your screen. Don't worry about the different categories that appear beneath the main selection of GuruFocus.com. At this time, you need to go to the homepage and clicking "GuroFocus.com" will take you to it. Once you are at the homepage, locate the menu at the top of the page. Click on the "Screener" selection and an expanded menu will be displayed. Scroll down the expanded menu, staying in the left column until you come to "DCF (&Reverse) Calculator" and click on it. Doing so will bring you to the Fair Value Calculator. It's the same thing as a DCF calculator but they have just given it a different name here. Because it's a great calculator but not the main one that I use, I won't spend any more time writing or talking about it. I will attempt to do a good job explaining my favorite DCF calculator to you next. Once you learn how to use it, you will find that the instructions also apply to this calculator.

Without a doubt, the DCF calculator found at Moneychimp.com is easily the best calculator that I have been able to find on the internet. It's absolutely marvelous and doesn't cost one penny to use. First, go online using Google or another web browser of your choice. Once at the browser, type "moneychimp.com" into the search portal of the browser and click the "search" button and "Moneychimp: Stock Market Investing, Online Calculators..." should appear as the first selection on your screen. Click on it and a screen should appear that brings you to another web page that contains several selections. On the right side of that page, you will find the category

How Much are Stocks Worth. Click on the *How Much are Stocks Worth* to go to that page. Once you are at that particular page, look to the right side of it and you will see a box titled "Article." Locate the "DCF Calculator" selection within the box and click on it to bring up the DCF calculator. The online calculator will look similar to the one in the example that follows:

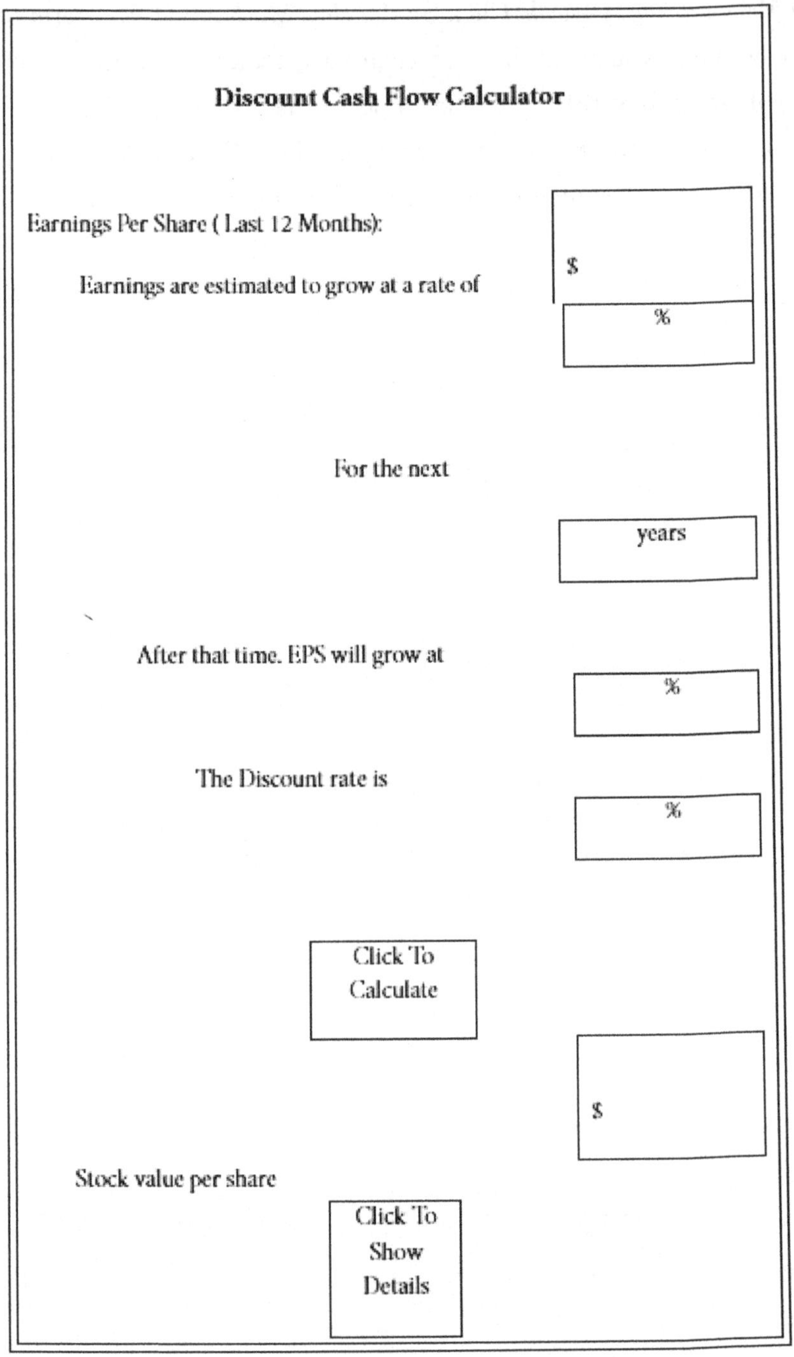

When using the DCF calculator, you will simply be inputting the required information into the calculator. Here's the information that will be needed to use the calculator:

Earnings Per Share (EPS): This is the total amount that the stock earned in the last twelve months or last annual reporting period.

Expected Earnings Per Share Growth Rate: This is the estimated rate at which earnings are expected to grow over a specific period of time.

Expected Time Period: This is the specific period of time that the future earnings per share estimates cover. I use ten years for the time period.

Leveling Off Period: After EPS have grown more rapid over a specific period of time, they are expected to level off at a lower rate of growth known as the leveling off period. Since I limit my future estimates to a period of ten years; I am not concerned about this leveling off period. My answer to it is always 0%. (zero percent).

Discount Rate: This is the rate by which we will discount future earnings. I always use a default rate of 5%. It is a rate that I established several years ago that's currently much higher than the 10 Year U.S. Treasury Note's yield. The 10 Year U.S. Treasury Note is considered by most financial experts to be the safest investment there is and the perfect yardstick to which other investments should be compared. Once the Treasury Note's yield surpasses 5%, I will use its higher yield as my discount rate. I don't think that we will see rates anywhere near 5% for many years to come. As I write, the yield on the 10 Year U.S. Treasury Notes stands at 2.43%. I have some older stock reports that I will be using to explain how I use the DCF Method to value a stock. The results obtained from the older reports will allow us to compare the estimates to the actual results that were obtained several years later. So, let's begin.

Let's start by taking a look at Middleby Corporation. Middleby Corporation is engaged in the design, manufacture, marketing, distribution, and service of a line of cooking and warming equipment used in commercial restaurants, institutional kitchens, and numerous other food industries. Looking at Middleby's 2009 stock report, we find that it was trading for $44.27 per share. It had managed to grow its earnings per share by more than 30% annually from 2004-2008 and analysts estimated that it would grow its EPS by 18.3% annually over the next five years. When determining which future EPS growth rate estimate to use, I compare the EPS growth that the stock has achieved for its most recent five-year period to the analysts' future EPS growth rate estimate and use the lower estimate of the two. Since analysts estimated Middleby's future EPS growth rate to be 18.3%, that's the rate that we will use as our long-term estimate for the next ten years.

MIDDLEBY (MIDD)EARNINGS PER SHARE 1999-2008

YEAR	1999	2000	2001	2002	2003	2004	2005	2006	2007	2008
EPS	0.05	0.19	0.09	0.33	1.00	1.19	1.99	2.57	3.11	3.75

Please note the consistency of Middleby's increases in its EPS for the ten-year period displayed. This is the type of consistency that I look for in every stock that I purchase. I will be putting the DCF calculator up for the first example but will only display the results of the calculator for the other examples that are given. Putting the information for Middleby Corporation into the DCF calculator will look like the following example:

Discount Cash Flow Calculator

Earnings Per Share (Last 12 Months):	$3.75
Earnings are estimated to grow at a rate of	18.3 %
For the next	10 years
After that time. EPS will grow at	0 %
The Discount Rate is	5.0 %
Click To Calculate	
Stock value per share	$
Click To Show Details	

After the information has been entered into the calculator, click the "Calculate" selection and the stock value per share will appear in its respective box as in the following example:

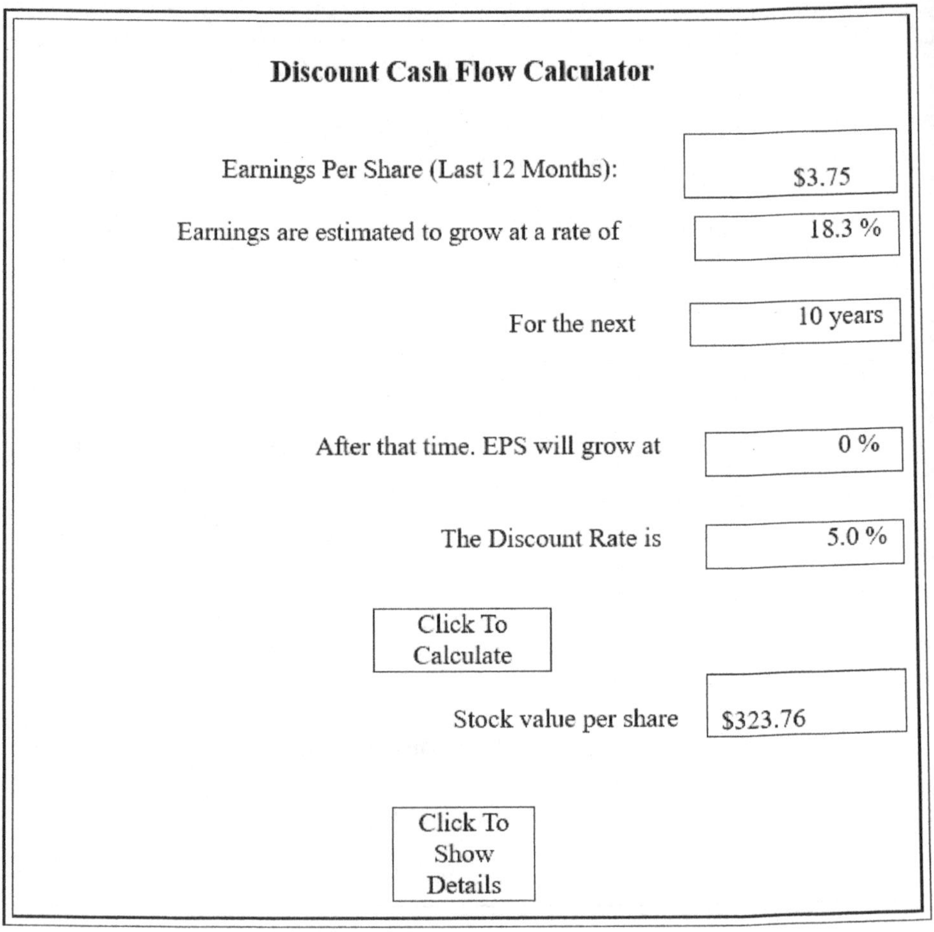

It's important that you not use the figure that appears in the "Stock value per share" box here because there are some additional calculations that are taking place that result in the higher stock value per share. I think that the calculation is actually the result of the software program attempting to calculate all future earnings beyond the ten-year period. Now, here is where Moneychimp's DCF calculator is head and shoulders above the rest and why I like it so much. Notice that the calculator has a "Show Details" button at the bottom of it. When we click on it, a table similar to the following one will appear and it's the bread and butter of the DCF Method:

MIDDLEBY CORPORATION'S
EPS ESTIMATES 2009-2018

YEAR	EARNINGS	PRESENT VALUE
1	4.44	4.23
2	5.25	4.76
3	6.21	5.36
4	7.34	6.04
5	8.69	6.81
6	10.28	7.67
7	12.16	8.64
8	14.38	9.73
9	17.02	10.97
10	20.13	12.36

The first column refers to future years. The center column is the actual earnings per share expected to be earned by a specific business, and the last column are those same earnings after a discount rate has been applied to them. Referring back to Middleby Corporation, these are the actual future earnings per share estimates based on the information that was entered into the DCF calculator. To determine the fair value or intrinsic value of Middleby Corporation, we need to refer to the "PRESENT VALUE" column and add up the total of those earnings. When we add those numbers up, we come up with a fair value or intrinsic value of $76.57 per share for Middleby Corporation. Again, referring to Middleby's 2009 stock report, we find that its stock was trading for $44.27 per share on November 3, 2009. At an estimated fair value of $76.57 per share, that means that we could have purchased Middleby Corporation at a discount of about 42% compared to its fair value estimate. I will only purchase a stock that can be bought at a minimum discount of 25% of its estimated fair value. That means that I would have looked to purchase Middleby Corporation when it was trading for $57.43 or less per share. Since it was trading at $44.27 per share, we can see that it was clearly a buy at the time. I initially performed this calculation on Memorial Day, May 26, 2014. Middleby Corporation's stock closed at a trading price of $234.17 on Friday, May 23, 2014. A purchase of Middleby Corporation for $44.27 per share on November 3, 2009, would have resulted in a total return of about 429% and an annual return rate of 43.8% at its trading price of $234.17 per share.

Next, we will take a look at Varian Medical Systems Incorporated. Varian Medical Systems designs, manufactures, sells, and services a variety of medical equipment and software products used in the treatment of cancer and a multitude of other medical applications. Looking at Varian Medical System's 2009 stock report, we find that it was trading for $40.66 per share. Varian Medical Systems had also managed to grow its earnings per share at an annual rate of 20% from 2005-2009 and analyst estimated that it would grow its EPS at an annual rate of 14.5% over the next five years. Since the analysts' estimate is lower than the historical rate of 20%, we will use their estimate. Here is a glimpse at Varian Medical Systems' earnings per share from 2000-2009.

VARIAN MEDICAL SYSTEMS INC. (VAR) EARNINGS PER SHARE 2000-2009

YEAR	2000	2001	2002	2003	2004	2005	2006	2007	2008	2009
EPS	0.07	0.41	0.50	0.67	0.92	1.18	1.50	1.80	1.86	2.31

Again, please note how Varian Medical Systems' has managed to increase its EPS over the 2000-2009 period consistently. Although we concentrate on five-year numbers for estimating the future EPS growth rate, we still want to see a seven to ten-year history of EPS that are consistently increasing like those of Varian Medical Systems Inc. To come up with our estimate of Varian Medical Systems' fair value, we must input the following information into the DCF calculator.

Earnings Per Share (Last 12 Months): $2.31

Earnings are estimated to grow at a rate of 14.5%

For the next 10 years

After that time, EPS will grow at 0%

The Discount Rate is 5% (minimum)

After the information has been entered into the calculator, click the "Calculate" selection and the stock value per share will appear in its respective box. Remember not to use the figure that appears in the "Stock value per share" box. Click on the "Show Details" button to pull up the DCF table of future EPS estimates. Here are the results for Varian Medical Systems Inc.:

VARIAN MEDICAL SYSTEMS INC
EPS ESTIMATES 2010-2019

YEAR	EARNINGS	PRESENT VALUE
1	2.64	2.51
2	3.03	2.75
3	3.47	3.00
4	3.97	3.27
5	4.55	3.57
6	5.21	3.89
7	5.96	4.24
8	6.82	4.62
9	7.81	5.03
10	8.95	5.49

To determine the fair value or intrinsic value of Varian Medical Systems Inc., we need to refer to the "PRESENT VALUE" column and add up the total of those earnings. When we add those numbers up, we come up with a fair value or intrinsic value of $38.37 per share for Varian Medical Systems Inc. Referring to Varian Medical Systems' 2009 stock report, we find that its stock was trading for $40.66 per share on August 24, 2009. With our 25% discount rule, we would have needed to purchase Varian Medical Systems at an average price of $28.78 per share. At its trading price of $38.37, it would have been way too expensive for me. Let's see how we would have done if we chose to purchase Varian Medical Systems Inc. at the price of $40.66 per share back in August of 2009. Varian Medical Systems' stock closed at a trading price of $80.92 on Friday, May 23, 2014. A purchase of Varian Medical Systems for $40.66 per share would have resulted in a total return of about 99% and an annual return rate of 15.3% which would have still been good, but we need the additional margin of safety with every purchase that we make. If we could have purchased Varian Medical Systems at our desired price, our annual return rate would have been 23.5%. What a difference that would have made!

We will look at one last company using the DCF Method and YUM! Brands Incorporated is it. Like most of us, I'm sure that you have visited KFC, Pizza Hut, Taco Bell, or some other restaurant that belongs to YUM! Brands Inc. Yum! Brands Inc. is a very big business and its current market capitalization stands at more than 31 billion dollars. Does the DCF Method work for it since it's such a big company? Let's see what kind of numbers we come up with using the DCF Method. Looking at YUM! Brands 2011 stock report, we find that it was trading for $57.50 per share. It had managed to grow its earnings per share by 13.9% annually from 2006-2010 and analysts estimated that it would grow its EPS by 11.4% over the next five years. Since the lower of the two estimates is 11.4%, that's the number that we will use. Here is the table of YUM! Brands historical EPS and the table of the result of the DCF calculator:

YUM! BRANDS INC. (YUM)EARNINGS PER SHARE 2001-2010

YEAR	2001	2002	2003	2004	2005	2006	2007	2008	2009	2010
EPS	0.81	0.94	1.01	1.21	1.28	1.46	1.68	1.96	2.22	2.38

YUM! BRANDS INC.

EPS ESTIMATES 2011-2020

YEAR	EARNINGS	PRESENT VALUE
1	2.65	2.52
2	2.95	2.68
3	3.29	2.84
4	3.67	3.02
5	4.08	3.20
6	4.55	3.40
7	5.07	3.60
8	5.64	3.82
9	6.29	4.05
10	7.01	4.30

To determine the fair value or intrinsic value of YUM! Brands Inc., refer to the "PRESENT VALUE" column and add up the total of the earnings from the "PRESENT VALUE" column. We come up with a fair value or intrinsic value of $33.43 per share for YUM! Brands Inc. If we base our purchase on YUM! Brands' trading price of $57.50 on December 16, 2011, YUM! Brands would have been too expensive for our purchase. Is the $33.43 a fair assessment of YUM! Brands real value because it's such a large company with a solid history of positive growth and solid performance? That's a question that every investor must answer for himself or herself and the answers come more naturally with practice. Here's my answer. I think that the $33.43 was a fair estimate of YUM! Brands intrinsic value at that time. Also remember that in actuality, we still needed to discount YUM! Brands' fair value by 25% before purchasing it. Upon checking, I found that YUM! Brands Inc., closed at a trading price of $76.17 on Tuesday, May 27, 2014. If we had gone ahead and purchased YUM! Brands although it appeared to be overvalued according to the DCF Method, we would have earned a total return of 32.5% and an annual return rate of 11.9% for the period. So, based on YUM! Brands Inc. performance, we would have been smart to stay away from it as a purchase unless we are satisfied with the return and don't think that we can do much better.

I told you earlier that I no longer perform DCF calculations by hand and that's true. So, it was my intention not to bother explaining to you how to perform DCF calculations by hand because the process is time-consuming. I'm very thankful to the inventor or inventors of the online DCF calculators that I have come to rely on. Nevertheless, I have decided to show you how to perform DCF calculations by hand in the same manner that I use too. I figured that if I didn't show you, I would probably end up beating myself up later for failing to do so. Let's begin by looking again at Varian Medical Systems Inc. financial information that was contained in its 2009 stock report. According to the report, Varian Medical Systems earned $2.31 in 2009 and its EPS were estimated to grow at a long-term annual rate of 14.5% The financial information needed to perform the calculation follows:

The Earnings Per Share (Last 12 Months): $2.31

Earnings are estimated to grow at a rate of 14.5%

For the next 10 years

Discount Rate is 5% (minimum)

First, we need to estimate our annual EPS for the next ten years. With this method, a regular calculator will suffice. It's my intention to keep things simple when using this method. Here's how and what needs to be entered into the calculator to estimate the EPS based on Varian Medical Systems financial information.

2.31 + 14.5% = 2.64 + 14.5% = 3.03 + 14.5% = 3.47 + 14.5% = 3.97 + 14.5% = 4.55 + 14.5% = 5.21 + 14.5% = 5.96 + 14.5% = 6.82 + 14.5% = 7.81 + 14.5% = 8.95

The arithmetic was continued in the preceding example until there were enough EPS estimates for ten future years. After the EPS estimates are calculated, each year's EPS estimate must be discounted for risk. In the following example, those discounted EPS estimates are located in the Present Value column. I used the discount rate of 5% which becomes a discount factor of 1.05 when being used to discount future earnings. In order to discount each year's EPS estimate, the EPS estimate must be divided by the discount rate/factor for each year.

YEAR	Future EPS Est.	Divided By Discount Rate			Present Value
1	$2.64	1.05			$2.51
2	$3.03	$(1.05)^2$	OR	1.103	$2.75
3	$3.47	$(1.05)^3$	OR	1.158	$3.00
4	$3.97	$(1.05)^4$	OR	1.216	$3.26
5	$4.55	$(1.05)^5$	OR	1.276	$3.57
6	$5.21	$(1.05)^6$	OR	1.340	$3.89
7	$5.96	$(1.05)^7$	OR	1.407	$4.24
8	$6.82	$(1.05)^8$	OR	1.477	$4.62
9	$7.81	$(1.05)^9$	OR	1.551	$5.04
10	$8.95	$(1.05)^{10}$	OR	1.629	$5.49
		Intrinsic/Fair Value			$38.37

By adding up the annual EPS estimates contained in the "Present Value" column, the intrinsic/fair value is obtained. If you were to go back and check the fair value estimate provided by the online DCF calculator and compare it to the value that I calculated by hand, you will see that they were both $38.37. That lets us know that both methods definitely work in the same manner to determine the fair value of a stock. As I said earlier, the only drawback to performing DCF calculation by hand is the fact that the process takes much longer to complete than using an online DCF calculator. Before we wrap things up, let's look at one more example of how to perform DCF calculations by hand. In the next example that's provided, the financial information has been fabricated.

Earnings Per Share (Last 12 Months): $4.38

Earnings are estimated to grow at a rate of 18.0%

For the next 10 years

The Discount Rate is 12%

To start, we need to estimate our annual EPS for the next ten years then complete the rest of the process like we did in the previous example. The discount rate of 12% becomes a discount factor of 1.12 in the example that follows:

4.38 + 18.0% = 5.17 + 18.0% = 6.10 + 18.0% = 7.20 + 18.0% = 8.49 + 18.0% = 10.02

+ 18.0% = 11.82 + 18.0% = 13.95 + 18.0% = 16.46 + 18.0% = 19.43 + 18.0% = 22.92

YEAR	Future EPS Est.	Divided By Discount Rate			Present Value
1	$5.17	1.12			$4.62
2	$6.10	$(1.12)^2$	OR	1.254	$4.86
3	$7.20	$(1.12)^3$	OR	1.405	$5.12
4	$8.49	$(1.12)^4$	OR	1.574	$5.39
5	$10.02	$(1.12)^5$	OR	1.762	$5.69
6	$11.82	$(1.12)^6$	OR	1.974	$5.99
7	$13.95	$(1.12)^7$	OR	2.211	$6.31
8	$16.46	$(1.12)^8$	OR	2.476	$6.65
9	$19.43	$(1.12)^9$	OR	2.733	$7.11
10	$22.92	$(1.12)^{10}$	OR	3.106	$7.38
			Intrinsic/Fair Value		$38.37

Again, add up the annual EPS estimates contained in the "Present Value" column to determine the stock's fair value which is $38.37 in the preceding example. I used this hand method for several years before discovering the online DCF calculators. As you can probably see, the DCF calculators make performing DCF calculations a lot easier and quicker. If you find that you are a little intimidated because the DCF Method seems complex, don't worry. Knowing how to calculate it by hand isn't necessary since the online calculators will do so for us. I wanted to at least explain the method for those that may be interested in its use. Don't forget to check out the excellent DCF calculator at Gurufocus.com that gives you very accurate estimates of fair or intrinsic value also. Again, all you have to do is enter the financial information that's needed into the calculator.

USING MONEYCHIMP'S GRAHAM STYLE FORMULA TO VALUE A STOCK

Benjamin Graham is without a doubt one of the most influential and intelligent investors to have ever lived. It's the knowledge that he shared with his students that has resulted in them achieving the amazing success that they have. Graham's most famous and best-known pupil is none other than Warren Buffett. Graham was continuously searching for a better way to quickly and easily place a value on a stock or company and created many formulas for just that purpose.

In his book The *Intelligent Investor,* Graham provides a formula for determining the value of growth stocks. I like the fact that the formula is simple to use. Because the formula was developed many, many years ago, it tends to provide valuations that are very high by today's standards. There's no doubt that the original formula worked for Graham but because things have changed somewhat, it was necessary for some modification to the original formula to brings modern stock valuations into what appears to be a more reasonable valuation range. Here is the original formula:

Value = Current Earnings x (8.5 plus twice the expected annual growth rate)

Since I don't use the original formula, I won't bother going into details to explain it. The modified equation that I adopted from MoneyChimp.com produces more conservative valuations than Graham's original formula and it's the actual formula that I use and it follows:

P/E = 9 + (0.5 X Growth Rate)

Or

Fair Value = 9 + (0.5 X Estimated EPS Growth Rate)

I'm going to show you how I use the preceding formula and it has worked very well for me. Always remember that others may use it differently and that's okay if that is what works for them, but what I'm showing you is how I now use it. We will do a valuation using the three stocks that were used earlier in the DCF Method examples. Let's begin.

Looking at Middleby's 2009 stock report, we find that it was trading for $44.27 per share. It had managed to grow its earnings per share by more than 30% from 2004-2008 and analysts estimated that it would grow its EPS by 18.3% over the next five years. Since analysts estimated Middleby's future EPS growth rate to be 18.3%, that's the rate that we will use for our calculation. Analysts also estimated that Middleby would earn $3.24 per share in 2009. Here's what the Graham Style Formula from MoneyChimp.com would look like with those figures plugged into it.

P/E = 9 + (0.5 X Estimated EPS Growth Rate)

P/E = 9 + (0.5 X 18.3)

P/E = 9 + 9.15

P/E = 18.15

After the P/E has been determined for a stock, multiply the P/E by the estimated EPS for 2009. It will be as follows:

$3.24 (2009 EPS Estimate) x 18.15 (Graham Formula P/E) = $58.81 (Fair

Value)

Next, as with the DCF Method that was shown, I discount the fair value by 25% to determine my purchase price for Middleby Corporation.

$58.81 (Fair Value) X .75 (Discount Multiple) = $44.11 (Purchase Price)

Middleby Corporation was trading for $44.27 at the time and my purchase price would have been $44.11. Because there is such a small difference between the two values, I would not have hesitated to buy Middleby Corporation at its $44.27 trading price.

Let's check out Varian Medical Systems next. Looking at Varian Medical System's 2009 stock report, we find that it was trading for $40.66 per share. Varian Medical System had also managed to grow its earnings per share at an annual rate of 20% from 2005-2009 and analyst estimated that it would grow its EPS at an annual rate of 14.5% over the next five years. Since the analysts' estimate was lower than the historical rate of 20%, we will use their estimate for the calculation. Analysts also estimated that Varian Medical Systems would earn $2.62 per share in 2010.

Here's the result of the Graham Style Formula from MoneyChimp.com with those figures plugged into it.

P/E = 9 + (0.5 X Estimated EPS Growth Rate)

P/E = 9 + (0.5 X 14.5)

P/E = 16.25

$2.62 (2010 EPS Estimate) x 16.25 (Graham Formula P/E) = $42.58 (Fair Value)

$42.58 (Fair Value) X .75 (Discount Multiple) = $31.94 (Purchase Price)

Varian Medical Systems was trading for $40.66 at the time and our purchase price would have been $31.94. Under the Graham Style Formula, you can clearly see that Varian Medical Systems Inc. was way too expensive for us and definitely should not have been bought.

Now, we will look at YUM! Brands Inc. using this method. Looking at YUM! Brands Inc.'s 2011 stock report, we find that it was trading for $57.50 per share. It had managed to grow its earnings per share by 13.9% from 2006-2010 and analysts estimated that it would grow its EPS by 11.4% over the next five years. Since the lowest of the two estimates was 11.4%, that's the number that we will use. Analysts also estimated that YUM! Brands Inc.'s EPS would be $2.86 per share for 2011. Here are the calculations for YUM! Brands Inc.:

P/E = 9 + (0.5 X Estimated EPS Growth Rate)

P/E = 9 + (0.5 X 11.4)

P/E = 14.7

$2.86 (2011 EPS Estimate) x 14.70 (Graham Formula P/E) = $42.04 (Fair Value)

$42.04 (Fair Value) X .75 (Discount Multiple) = $31.53 (Purchase Price)

YUM! Brands was trading for $57.50 per share and we needed to purchase it at $31.53 per share or less according to the formula which includes the margin of safety. As with Varian Medical Systems Inc., YUM! Brands Inc. is another stock that would have been too expensive for our purchase.

MoneyChimp.com is an amazingly informative web site and I highly recommend that you visit it. The site also contains many other useful tools that I bet that you will find of great value such as the compound interest calculator that lets you figure out different growth rates. MoneyChimp has surely made investing a lot easier for me and it has done so without any cost to me. Now, what can be better than that except for free money!

SUMMARY OF FAIR VALUE ESTIMATES

STOCK'S NAME & INFO.	DISCOUNT CASH FLOW METHOD	MONEYCHIMP'S GRAHAM STYLE FORMULA
MIDDLEBY CORP. 2009 EPS EST. $3.24 EPS GR. RATE EST. 18.3%	$76.57	$58.81
VARIAN MEDICAL 2010 EPS EST. $2.62 EPS GR. RATE EST. 14.5%	$44.00	$42.58
YUM! BRANDS INC. 2011 EPS EST. $2.86 EPS GR. RATE EST. 11.4%	$33.43	$42.04

The preceding table shows the intrinsic values or estimated fair values for each of the stocks that have been discussed using the two methods discussed. Only the analysts' estimates were used during the valuing process because they were lower than the historical growth rates. By using the lower estimates, you will pay less for a stock, not more. The only drawback of using the lower estimates is the fact that stocks must be cheaper before being purchased compared to using higher estimates which could keep you or me from buying some stocks. That's it. Remember, by paying less for a stock, you lower your risk and increase your chance of making a higher return. Also remember, the estimates given in the preceding table are for information purpose only and the values are outdated and no longer relevant.

USE LIMIT ORDERS WHEN BUYING OR SELLING STOCKS

There are several types of orders that can be placed when we buy or sell a stock but it's my belief that the individual or small investor needs only an understanding of two types, and they are *market orders* and *limit orders.*

A market order is defined as an order to buy or sell a stock at the best available price. With market orders, the order is generally executed quickly but the drawback is that the price at which a market order will be executed is not guaranteed. In other words, when using market orders, it is possible to pay more for a stock or receive less for a stock than you desire.

A limit order is defined as an order to buy or sell a stock at a specific price or better. The drawback to using limit orders is that it can only be filled if the stock market's price reaches the limit price and the numbers of shares desired are available for purchase. The advantage of using limit orders is that they prevent an investor from paying more than he or she desires for a stock being purchased and guarantee that he or she will receive the price desired or a better one for the stock that is being sold if the trade executes.

In the past, I have used both types of orders but now believe that an investor is always better off using limit orders when buying or selling shares of any stocks through his or her brokerage account. In my mind, placing or using market orders is a losing proposition and is always to an investor's disadvantage. So, always use limit orders when buying and selling stocks. That way, the deal works in your favor instead of someone else's.

INVEST AS IF YOU'RE BUYING THE WHOLE BUSINESS

Before investing in a stock, I like to get an idea of what my initial rate of return would be if I were buying the entire business. This step is a mental process or calculation that has become second nature for me when I'm researching a company or its stock. Remember, if you currently own stocks, you are already a business owner. Each share of stock that you own entitles you to ownership of a small percentage of the business, and thereby, a share in the profits or losses generated by the business.

Because you are a business owner, you must think and act like an owner, but that process should start long before you invest your money into any business or its stock. Part of that thinking process is to ask yourself WRII-FM. When I first saw those initials, I thought that they were identifiers of a radio station, and I must admit that I was totally wrong! The initials WRII-FM really mean, "What's Really in It for Me?" Literally, that's a question that every investor should ask himself or herself. It may seem to be a selfish question to ask ourselves but it's our money that's on the line with every investment that we make, and I think that gives us the right to act a little selfish. Now let's return to the business owner part.

Since you invest in stocks that qualify you as a business owner, no intelligent person would ever intentional buy a business if there's nothing to be gained from its purchase, and I have never met anyone who invests in stocks that didn't want to make some money. So, one way to answer the WRII-FM question is by buying a stock at a discount to its fair or intrinsic value. Another way to answer that question is to see what our *initial rate of return* would be if we were buying the whole business. You and I should be asking that question regardless of whether or not we can actually afford to purchase the entire business. Here's why. Most of the great investors believe that to be a successful investor, one needs to understand how to value a business. When we, as investors, estimate the fair or intrinsic value of a stock, we are in reality attempting to value the business that issued the stock shares. Because we should be concerned with the overall performance of any business that's of interest to us, it makes perfect sense to estimate what our initial rate of return would be if we were buying the whole business. Why? If the whole business isn't worth buying, we have no business buying even one share of its stock. Doesn't that make sense?

There are only two numbers that I use to estimate the initial rate of return. They are the company's *current market capitalization* and its *net income* for the trailing twelve months (TTM). Even if a company fails to increase its net income by a large margin for the current year, there's at least the possibility that its net income will closely match or exceed the net income for the trailing twelve months. Let's just say that using the net income for the trailing twelve months is a kind of insurance policy. So, let's look at some examples of how to estimate the initial rate of return if we were buying the whole business.

First, we will take a look at AmTrust Financial Services Inc. According to a 2014 stock report for AmTrust Financial Services, its market capitalization stood at 2.91 billion dollars and its net income for the trailing twelve months was 345.6 million dollars at the time of the report's preparation. To determine the initial rate of return on the purchase of AmTrust Financial Services Inc., divide its net income (TTM) by its current market capitalization. Look at the example that follows:

Net Income (TTM) / Market Capitalization = Initial Rate Of Return

345.6 Million / 2.91 Billion = 11.8% Initial Rate Of Return

If we had bought the entire company of AmTrust Financial Services Inc., we would have been expecting an initial rate of return of 11.8% or better from our investment if the business performed as expected.

We will next look at Coach Inc., now known as Tapestry. At the time of the report in 2013, Coach traded at $55.55 per share. Its market capitalization was 14.2 billion dollars and its net income (TTM) was 1.05 billion dollars.

1.05 Billion / 14.2 Billion = 7.3% Initial Rate Of Return

A purchase of Coach Inc. should have netted us an initial rate of return of 7.3% or better on our purchase of the entire company. Shares of Coach Inc. eventually tumbled in price and began to trade at prices that I like and I bought shares for my newest portfolio when they traded in the $36 per share range.

We will look next at Discovery Holdings Company also known as Discovery Communications Inc., a global nonfiction media and entertainment company. I have taken a serious look at this business but have never bought any of its shares. I may add shares to at least one of my portfolios at some future date after I have thoroughly studied the company. Upon looking at a 2013 stock report for Discovery Holdings Co., I found out that it carried a market capitalization of 18.8 billion dollars and its net income (TTM) was 954 million dollars.

954 million / 18.8 Billion = 5.0% Initial Rate Of Return

Had we invested in Discovery Holding Co. at the time reported, we could have expected an initial rate of return of 5% or better if we bought the whole company and it performed as expected.

Let's look at one last company using this method and that company is Whole Foods Market Inc., which was bought by Amazon in 2017. Whole Foods Market sells natural and organic foods and is also a Certified Organic grocer. According to a 2014 stock report for Whole Foods Market, it had a market capitalization of 13.76 billion dollars and its net income (TTM) was 572 million dollars.

572 million / 13.76 Billion = 4.1% Initial Rate Of Return

We would have been expecting an initial rate of return of 4.1% or better from our purchase of Whole Foods Market had we bought the whole company and it performed as expected. This is the process that I use to get an idea of the initial rate of return to expect if a business is purchased in its entirety. I have noticed that with my own purchases, the initial rate of return tends to fall within the range of 10% but that's not always the case. With some of my purchases, the returns are lower and with others, they are a little higher

Although performing this calculation is not a necessity, I believe that its use is bound to help you and me to identify and buy stocks when they are trading at very good values. I have been using this calculation for a few years now and believe that my use of it along with my fair value estimate of a company's stock, gives me a better overall picture of WRII-FM. In the end, that's what matters most when it comes to investing. Don't you agree? I also want to mention that I prefer investing in those stocks that provide an initial rate of return of 10% or more.

WHEN TO SELL A STOCK

This section of the book was extracted in its entirety from my book titled *You Can Invest Like a Stock Market Pro.* I wrestled with the decision of whether or not to include it in this book, but in the end, I decided to do so. Mainly because determining when to sell a stock is a decision that even the world's best investors struggle with. For me, deciding when to buy a stock is a much easier decision than deciding when to sell it. That's a fact!

Warren Buffett has said that his holding period for a stock is forever. Does Buffett really hold every stock that he buys forever? Of course not! The point that he is making is that you should always purchase a stock with the intention of holding it forever; therefore, make sure that your money has been put into your best investment ideas. Author Robert Hagstrom has written several excellent books about Warren Buffett and his investment strategies. In *The Warren Buffett Portfolio,* he says that an investor should leave his or her portfolio intact for at least five years, as long as the fundamentals for which a specific stock was purchased do not deteriorate. He also says investors should pay no attention to a stock's price volatility because it is a normal part of the investment cycle. In their book *Million Dollar Portfolio,* the Motley Fool team says investors' minimum holding period for each stock that is purchased should be three to five years. As a long-term investor, there will be times when it makes sense to sell or reduce your position in a particular stock earlier than you had planned. Next, we will talk about different circumstances in which you should consider selling a stock or reducing your position in a stock.

The Time Frame - If you will need the money within five years, it should not be invested in stocks. It would be best to invest your money in safe and stable short-term instruments. Money market accounts, money market funds, and short-term certificates of deposits would be better options. Since the Great Recession struck, some investment professionals now recommend that you not invest any money in stocks that will be needed within 10 years.

An Overvalued Stock - When a stock is significantly overvalued, sell it. Take the proceeds from the sale and invest them into other undervalued stocks that you have researched. The P/E ratio is still one of the best indicators of value. For example, if a stock has traded at an average P/E of 15 for the last seven to 10 years and the business is thriving, but the stock currently trades at a P/E of 30 or more on consistent or increasing EPS, you should seriously consider selling the stock. The PEG ratio, explained in my first book, is also a very effective method for determining if a stock is now overvalued. I must admit that I'm slow to sell an overvalued stock if it's not extremely overvalued because excellent investment choices are hard to find and if they are in my portfolio, it's because I consider them to be excellent selections. When a stock is overvalued by 50%, I would not hesitate to sell it quickly in order to put my money into other investments that are of better value.

Too Much Debt - Too much debt is dangerous for any business because there's always the chance that a business may be unable to repay its debt. Too much debt also puts a business at greater risk of failure if a downturn in the industry or economy were to occur. Upon entering the 2007 recession, thousands of businesses here in the United States disappeared practically overnight and that was before things really got bad. I'm willing to bet that those businesses that were carrying too much debt were the first to go.

Too Much Risk - Sometimes new management will come to a business and begin to implement new policies; along with that implementation they will knowingly or unknowingly expose a business to greater risk. If you purchased the stock of a business that stayed away from risky practices, but the business has now begun to display risky behaviors that make you uncomfortable, sell the stock and find yourself a better investment.

Loss of Competitive Advantage - When a business changes its business model, resulting in it losing its competitive advantage, sell the stock. Having a durable competitive advantage is essential to any stock that you and I purchase if we are truly going to invest as the pros do.

The Portfolio Lacks Balance or Diversification - It's quite simple for your best performing stock to become the largest holding in your portfolio, and there's absolutely nothing wrong with that. The problem arises when the stock makes up more than 20-25% of your portfolio's total value. I would be very uncomfortable having more than 25% of my portfolio's value tied to just one stock. Legendary investor, Jim Slater suggests that individual investors limit the number of funds invested in a single stock within their portfolios to a maximum of 15%. When your portfolio becomes heavily weighted in one stock, consider reducing your position of that stock to bring more balance and better diversification into your portfolio.

Stock Reaches Its Fair Value – Our goal as investors should always be to purchase a stock at a discount to its fair value and I recommend at least a 25% discount to its fair value. By doing so, when you sell a stock that has reached its fair value, you are guaranteed a gain of at least 25% from the sell. This is a disciplined approach to selling a stock. According to research, it was common for Benjamin Graham to sell a stock once it had a 50% gain in price. If the future prospects of a particular stock look good, you may decide to sell only a portion of the stock such as half of its shares and hold on to the rest when using this approach.

When Your Analysis is Found to Be Flawed- There will be times when an investor will be very detailed and careful in his or her analysis of a particular company or its stock, only to find out later that his or her analysis is incorrect or flawed. Whether a stock should be sold at that time depends on the seriousness of the error and its impact on the long-term performance of the business. So, when you find that you have incorrectly analyzed a particular business, it is essential for you to take a serious look at all available information to determine whether or not to sell the stock or to continue holding it. One thing is certain, as an investor, you will not always be right when analyzing a company or its stock.

Based on my observation and research, I have not discovered a clear-cut way to determine the optimal time to sell a stock. There will be times that you will sell a stock because it has not performed well, only to see it skyrocket and double or triple in price soon after you sell it. There will also be occasions when you have purchased what seems to be the perfect stock, only to watch it tumble in price and for no apparent reason. Learn what you can from these events and move on. Even Peter Lynch, Jim Slater, and other great investors have sold stocks too early or too late. It's going to happen sometimes.

DEAR READER,

I really enjoyed sharing with you the knowledge that I have obtained through more than ten years of research, study, and portfolio management. If you have enjoyed this book and have a minute to spare, I would really appreciate a short review on the page or website from which you bought the book. Even if you didn't like it, I would enjoy your feedback. Reviews can be tough to come by these days. You, the reader, have the power to make or break a book. I would certainly appreciate it if you would go to Amazon and/or Goodreads and complete a short review of this work. I have provided the links for both Amazon and Goodreads, below. Thank you so much for reading *Now That You Can Invest Like a Pro.*

In gratitude,

James Pattersenn Jr.

Amazon Link: https://www.amazon.com/James-Pattersenn-Jr./e/B07GBMFKQ2/ref=ntt_dp_epwbk_0

Goodreads Link: https://www.goodreads.com/book/show/41387633-you-can-invest-like-a-stock-market-pro

OTHER BOOKS BY THE AUTHOR

You Can Invest Like A Stock Market Pro: How to Use Simple and Powerful Strategies of the World's Greatest Investors to Build Wealth

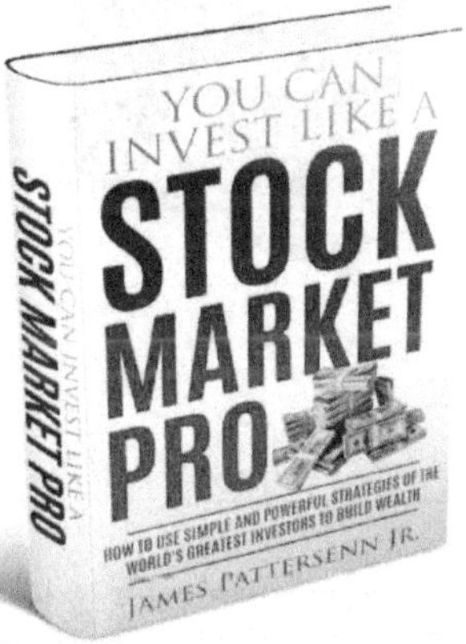

https://www.amazon.com/dp/B07G9PW4F2

Book available at www.howtoinvestinstocks.org, Amazon, major bookstores, and other online retailers. Available in Kindle, EPUB, PDF and Printed format

100 Stocks That a Young Warren Buffett Might Buy:

If He Invested Like He Does Today

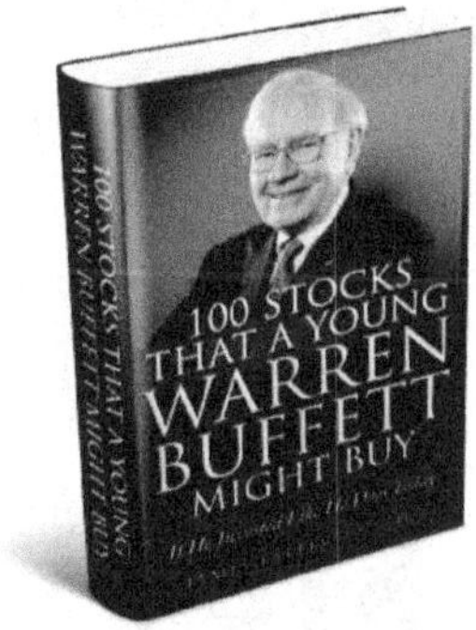

https://www.amazon.com/dp/B07T7XFQNW

Book available at Amazon, major bookstores, and other online retailers.

Available in Kindle and Printed format

ACKNOWLEDGEMENTS

My sincere thanks to:

Carrie Pattersenn, my sweet and unselfish mother. She taught me the importance of putting the needs of others before my own, if I truly wanted to be blessed and to be a blessing.

The great investors who have made this book possible because they cared enough to willingly share their wisdom and knowledge about investing with the rest of us.

Angie, a professional graphic designer, whom I found at Fiverr (the world's largest freelance services marketplace). She does amazing work, and you are going to love her prices! She can be contacted at "pro_ebookcovers", at the Fiverr website. If you need an eBook cover or printed book cover, hire her.

Most of all, I thank God, the Father, and my Lord Jesus Christ, who is gracious and merciful to all.

Indiex

Made in the USA
Monee, IL
04 November 2026

67384429R00059